The Power Bible

By

William Beteet III & Brendon Lemon

THE POWER BIBLE

ISBN # 978-0-578-60503-6
Library of Congress Control Number:2019917937

Published 2019 by Kwiggz-Cortez Publishing LLC
Cover design by Dylan Sowle, dylansowle.com
Editing by Juvian Hernandez, Brendon Lemon & William Beteet III

I dedicate this book to the woman who had the power to bring me into this world and the man who's always had the power to take me out of it.
- Will

I dedicate this book to my grandfather, who had the power to beat alcoholism, raise a family, all while being the sweetest man who anyone in his family had ever met. You showed us all how to be good men, Papa.
- Brendon

Contents

Foreword

I was scared someone was going to steal a lot of money from me.

I was having a problem in a negotiation. In fact, I was terrified that a group I was doing business with wasn't going to pay me what they owed me. I couldn't sleep. It was a big amount and I was obsessed with this. So I wanted to do a negotiation where they could pay me earlier than the scheduled date.

I had gone broke so many times before it was almost like I had post-traumatic stress that I was going to get ripped off. I couldn't function.

I needed help. That's when I called the authors of this book.

A week later, I was wired the money I negotiated for.

Another time, I was in a relationship where I didn't really understand what was happening. Why was she always mad at me? Why did I always have to defend myself when I wasn't even really sure what the underlying problems were.

Again, I called Bill and Brendon. Bill is a one-time lawyer, one time dating coach, part-time comedian. As Scott Adams, author of Dilbert, might say about such a situation: Bill had a great "talent stack" to have a unique perspective on persuasion. (lawyer skills + dating coach skills + comedian skills = a unique set of persuasion skills. Add to that Brendon's skills in sales.)

Actually, it's not persuasion. Bill and Brendon call it "frame control."

The Power Bible

"Spending energy 'trying to convince' others only strengthens their frame"

Bill told me, "In every high stakes situation, one person has the frame and the rest in the room does not. If you are a comedian, you're the one on the stage. If the audience takes the frame away from you (if you get nervous in the middle of a joke or stumble on a punchline and don't have a quick recovery) you will never get it back and that's the end of your show.

"If you lose the frame in a legal case to the other lawyer, you're going to lose the case, and if you lose the frame when you are asking out someone, you will lose status and chances are it won't work out.

"You can't constantly control the frame or the people around you will get 'frame fatigue'", he told me once. "But the key is to be aware of the frame so that when you need to take control of it, you can."

I would call him with many situations in my life and we'd walk through it and figure out who had the frame and who didn't and how could I make the situation work for me.

Sometimes he would be so accurate it was unreal.

"Be aware of your inferiority narratives"

Like if I was in an argument he would say, "try X, then you will see the other person do Y, then do Z, and you will see the other person do A or B and then you have to just be quiet and the other person will do C, and then you can do D".

"That's pretty specific," I would tell him. "Just do it," he would reply, and it would be uncanny how dead-on he was with each part of the interaction.

Perhaps because I had used his knowledge so many times over the years, they asked me to write the foreword for their book, The Power Bible.

I've read many books on persuasion. I've had many of the authors of those books on my podcast. I've interviewed the best in the world on negotiation, sales, the neuroscience of persuasion, cognitive biases, motivation, even hypnotism.

In every situation in life, there will be people who you need to persuade. In the past, hierarchies were created for us: you had a boss, or a professor, or other gatekeepers in life who tried to dictate your rules. But the rules have turned upside-down and it's only our ability to understand frame, and master the internal and external barriers for taking control of that frame that will carry us forward now into success, into pursuing our dreams, into creating meaning in our lives.

With frame control, as I have seen in my own life, others will have never seen someone like you before, someone who so quickly moves from the bottom, seemingly out of nowhere, and shoots their way to a top of a skill or industry.

"If you think you absolutely MUST say 'yes,' then that is a sign you absolutely need to say 'No.'"

The currency of this next century is your ability to not only have a unique vision and perspective, but to be able to persuade people of that vision, to be able to enlist the colleagues and partners you need to achieve your life goals.

When I read The Power Bible, I couldn't believe it. After starting so many businesses where I needed these tactics, and interviewing so many of the world's best, here was finally a book that gave real, actionable advice. Not just the results of scientific studies, or generic self-help advice that is regurgitated in every self-help book.

I'm not writing this foreword to help them sell books or to say "this book is great, I'm so glad I read it."

I've lived this book. Everything written here I have used and they've saved my life. They say, "Only the good players are lucky." And I've been very lucky. But only because I've used what you are about to read to get myself into situations that would have been very difficult to navigate if I didn't know about Frame Control.

On a stage speaking in front of hundreds of people, in personal situations, in business situations with millions at stake – it's like having a super power when you understand who has the frame, what actions are the keys to unlocking that frame and then, as I need it, taking control of that frame myself.

And it's not just about "use this word" or "mimic their behavior" or "get them to say a number first" and all the other BS pieces of advice in generic books on persuasion stolen from Wikipedia pages and overly-academic papers with no practical use.

The core of The Power Bible is how to light the mastery and confidence in yourself, at a deep internal level. And using that confidence outwards to clearly see the various frames and agendas being used by the people around you. Everyone has a "good reason" for their actions and words, and a "real reason." Being able to translate the "real reason" that is buried deep underneath the costume party of the world around us, is the beginning of developing your own powers in frame control.

Bill and Brendon, once again, I apologize for all the times I had to ask for your advice. All the times I had to say, "Well then he said this in the negotiation and I wasn't sure what…": or "Why do you think she said this and what can I do now to….?"

But I had to do it. And all your advice worked. I learned about Frame Control. Or at least I thought I did.

Until I realized how much was still left to learn.

Until I read this book.

- James Altucher

Prologue

Prologue

To be weak and perceived as powerful is more advantageous than being powerful but perceived as weak.

γνῶθι σεαυτόν

If you've come to this book, you have a desire. Perhaps it's the desire to better your life, perhaps it's the desire to improve the lives of those you love, or perhaps it's the desire to exact revenge against a world you feel is unjust; whatever the reason is, this book is a discussion of how to harness your power and influence others.

At times you may find yourself arguing against this book. At times you'll find yourself wishing that parts of it *weren't* true. At times, you'll disagree, but you'll know in your bones that what you read is the truth. Know that if this is you, you are the reader The Power Bible is for.

From here, go brilliantly and remember the words of Julius Caesar as brought to you by the bard "The fault, dear Brutus, is not in our stars, but in ourselves…"

Introduction

Introduction

To have power over another one must first have power over one's self. In order to have such power, one must have a framework to understand how power operates, individually and interpersonally, communally and sociologically.

It is for this reason The Power Bible begins with the exploration of the self before expanding outward to cover emotions, relationships, societies, subcultures and conversational dynamics.

Each topic introduced is meant to build on the insights from previous chapters. The Power Bible requires an active reader to make inferences on how the different concepts interact with one another, as your identity informs your emotions, your relationships are shaped by society, the subcultures you're a part of dictate the etiquette that control your conversations.

The Power Bible is an instrument to teach you how to win. To bend, disregard and strategically break the rules that bind you. Cultivating an awareness for which battles to fight, which ones to pass on, and how to win the moments that matter.

What follows is a dialogue presented the way Athenian philosophers would examine a topic. The speakers are our two authors.

Introduction to Inner Frame

The Power Bible

The Inner Frame

William: Your inner frame is your perception of yourself. It is the role that you believe you are supposed to play. Your inner frame is the most important frame because it governs your social instincts. Without a strong inner frame, your life will be dictated by the whims of others

Brendon: Without a strong personal frame you're going to find yourself accepting narratives from others, from the outside world, that *you* have not decided are the best for you

William: The world will give you a generalized role that is beneficial for *itself* but not necessarily beneficial for *you*.

Brendon: A personal frame is the foundational way that you operate and perceive in the world. As an example, if you're walking around somewhere and someone gives you a strange look, the way that you interpret that data without any additional information is going to be the default of your personal frame. So, if someone gives you a strange look and you have a strong, positive mental frame, then you will not perceive that look as an indicator that you are strange. Instead, your strong, positive mental frame will interpret that strange look as an indication that *they* are strange—that there is something about *them* that is wrong. Maybe you go, "Oh, do I have something on my shirt? Is there something going on behind me that I'm not aware of? Or, maybe that person just had a strange thought and happened to make eye contact."

In contrast, if you have a personal frame that states you are of low value and have to constantly try to win the affection of others, then you will interpret that same strange look negatively. Your internal narrative becomes "oh, something is wrong with me. I need to pick it up and dress better." Or, "I suck. I look weird. I'm ugly." Whatever that internal narrative happens to be, you internalize it in a negative way.

The key is to understand that your perception of the same scenario will

The Power Bible

change depending on the strength and positivity of your personal frame.

William: Your inner frame is constructed by your beliefs. Our beliefs become self-fulfilling prophecies. You will interact with the world in a way to assure that your beliefs are found to be true. If you do not believe that you are a person who deserves a good life, then you will act in a way where that guarantees that result.

There are five pillars that house your inner frame.

> <u>Respect</u>
> <u>Acceptance</u>
> <u>Conditioning</u>
> <u>Outcome Independence</u>
> <u>Context</u>

1 - Respect

William: If I told you I went to Harvard, you would probably have some unspoken respect for me. You would probably assume I am smart and hardworking. You might even find yourself deferring to me in conversation.

Now, what if I told you that I went to Harvard because my parents gave the university $15 million? Suddenly, your implicit respect vanishes. Why? I still went to Harvard, right?

Wrong. After learning that I paid my way in, you no longer perceive what I did as difficult. Respect is earned. So, we lose respect for those who took the easy route. The same goes for how we view ourselves. Our self-respect is derived from how often we do difficult tasks. How often are we putting ourselves in difficult situations and thriving?

Self-respect, however, is more than doing difficult tasks. For example, let's say one weekend I see Brendon picking up trash on the highway. I think to myself, "Wow! Look at Brendon doing community service. What an upstanding citizen. I respect that guy."

The Power Bible

Later, if I find out he was ordered to pick up trash on the highway by a judge as punishment for drinking and driving, his act now seems less impressive. That's because the court compelled him to do it, rather than his own personal passion for community service.

The same goes for how we come to respect ourselves. We feel self-respect when we are doing tasks that are both difficult and are done on our own volition. Our self-respect comes from actions, not rhetoric. For example, I cannot just say that I respect myself and magically respect myself. I must earn that respect through consistent action.

The more we respect ourselves, the more authority we have over ourselves. Self-authority is your ability to control your actions. The more you respect yourself, the better you will be at controlling your actions.

Just like a person you respect will have an easier time convincing you to do something than a person you don't. For example, soldiers march into enemy fire without question because they respect the commanding officer who gave the order.

This is why, after spending a weekend watching television, it's hard to get yourself to do something difficult, like go to the gym. Watching television is not a difficult task, so doing it for extended periods of time causes you to lose respect for yourself. The longer you sit around doing nothing, the less you respect yourself and the harder it will be to do tasks.

Actions → Respect → Authority → Actions

This chain is cyclical. The actions we take can either affect our self-respect in a negative or positive way. If it impacts our self-respect negatively then it lessens our ability to control our actions in the future, which leads to us carrying out worse actions.

The reverse is true. If an action impacts our self-respect positively, then it increases our ability to control our actions, which makes it easier for us to carry out better actions.

If you want to go run a marathon, the only way you can run a marathon is if you have enough respect for yourself to listen to your command to keep running. Emerson summed up the respect and authority concept when he said, "Do the thing and you shall have the power."

Self-control is the art of controlling your circumstance. The more you respect yourself the more you can control yourself. The more you can control your actions the faster you can transform your circumstance. You will also notice that the greater your ability to control yourself, the less others can control you.

The more you respect yourself the easier it will be to reject requests that don't align with your values. Saying *no* to others becomes easier when you are conditioned to say no to *yourself*. Remember, the more you control yourself, the less others can control you. This book is about forging your own destiny. The actions necessary to live an ideal life will often inconvenience others.

Others, with varying degrees of pressure, will try and take you off your path. Often, others do this by accident, not out of bad faith. It is just a result of your best life conflicting with their interests. Ironically, your ability to say no to opportunities, even good ones, is necessary to live an extraordinary life.

"No" is a lot harder to say when you don't respect yourself. This is because it's easier to go along with what other people are asking you to do. To say no, you need enough self-authority to say no and even more to follow through when you do say it. Both are hard if you don't respect yourself.

Also, people respect you less when you always say yes. To bring it back to the Harvard example, part of the reason why Harvard is such a respected institution is because it rejects so many applicants. If it were to say yes to every applicant it would destroy its reputation.

That being said, it's not enough just to reject people to earn their respect. Just like it takes more than self-denial to respect yourself.

You must create a person who is valuable as well. Harvard's low acceptance rate is only part of why it's well respected. The other reasons have to do with its world-renowned faculty, beautiful campus, and talented student body.

Part of the reason Harvard turns away so many applicants is because it cares about providing a valuable experience for its students. The Harvard experience is valuable because it, as an organization, for centuries, has done the difficult things, such as hiring elite faculty, building and maintaining a beautiful campus, and nurturing a strong, diverse student body. It would not be able to do any of these if it admitted every applicant.

Part of the reason Harvard was able to do this is because it has a mission that gives it an institutional identity. You as an individual have an identity too. For many, it remains a nebulous composition of personality traits and preferences with no organizing principle—no clear mission to help organize and refine their character. It is from this unorganized mess that many create their identity. Remember, if you do not choose a character, the world will pick one for you.

You must take action and choose your character.

It is best to draft this out. Think hard about your character, like in a video game. Outline what she wants out of life. What is his goal? Where would he need to live to accomplish this goal? What is standing in his way? What excuses does she not accept? What does he look like? What does he do on a daily basis? What kind of food does she eat? What does he do on the weekend? How does she waste time?

The person you outlined is the strongest version of yourself, he is an ideal you. This is the person you will be working towards. You can't start at the ideal because you do not have enough self-respect. Nor do you have enough self-authority to transform yourself overnight. Your transformation will take time and effort. This is why many people fail their New Year's resolutions.

You want to start small and make things more difficult only after you have earned it. A consistent daily schedule is the key. Each task and behavior should move you in the direction of your dreams. This is a hard process, but it should condition you to seek the reward of an improved life. It should be a reward, not a punishment—something earned, not given.

Respect for yourself has two cycles. There is (1) life respect, respect for the decisions you have made throughout your life, and (2) daily respect, respect for yourself that must be earned every day.

Cultivating habits that earn you daily respect will increase your life respect. In turn, the more respect you have for your life as a whole, the easier it will be to earn daily respect. Those with large amounts of life respect will be able to get back on track after a period of not earning daily respect. The less life respect you have, however, the harder it will be to sustain daily respect, and the harder it will be to get back on track after falling off course.

Living up to a realistic standard is called having self-awareness. You are not underestimating yourself, but at the same time you're not overestimating your resolve. This will increase your levels of self-respect and in turn your levels of self-authority and you can start a virtuous cycle.

The danger of not living up to your new standard is that it will be easier to descend into negative emotional states. Much of the general anxiety we experience in the morning when we wake up or when we are alone is from not living up to our standards. This causes us to sink into a vicious cycle of self-attack.

Disgust is the complete absence of respect.

Similar to how people will relentlessly attack someone they are disgusted by; we constantly do the same to ourselves. The more you squander your potential the louder the internal voice of disdain. If you stay in a state of self-disgust for long enough, you *will* descend into depression—having so little self-respect and self-authority that you don't even get out of bed.

People try to avoid these voices by self-medicating with drugs, sex, porn, or video games. Ironically, the longer you run away the louder the voices get. Until you fall deeper down the pit of addiction trying to run away from the voices in your head.

You might tell yourself that you enjoy the party life, but part of you knows that's a lie. Even though you might say that you are living in accordance with your values, your mind knows you could do so much more.

Your values are an important component of self-respect and differ among individuals. For example, an athlete might have a standard for themselves that values conditioning and strength. In order for them to have respect for themselves, they need to engage in activities that make them faster and stronger. On the other hand, an academic might have a standard for themselves that values writing and research. In order for them to respect themselves, they need to engage in activities that furthers their research or writing. Many people suffer from not knowing what they value or acting in a way that doesn't match their unspoken values.

Brendon: A lot of that occurs because they accept values from their social environments that they never decided for themselves. Part of the reason William mentioned that women and minorities sometimes find it difficult to have self-esteem is because they've accepted social narratives, a.k.a. stereotypes, claiming that they are of lesser value.

Some of these people have never decided to sit down and think to themselves, "How much do I value myself? How much do I respect myself? What are the values that I really want to believe in?" If they did, they might reject the culture around them. This rejection doesn't have to be reactive, it's just an activity, a decision, and after they do it, they can go on to pursue the lives they want for themselves.

Oprah Winfrey said you have to teach people how they need to treat you, and that's exactly what it means. But beyond even that, you have to teach yourself how you need to treat you.

William: Respect is earned, so it's not enough to set values for yourself and simply think, "How do I want to interact with the world?" You must take action. Each action that you take in the direction of your goals will make it easier for you to respect yourself, but that's only one piece of the puzzle.

Another important part of self-respect is your internal narrative. An Olympian acquaintance of mine won the silver medal in a highly publicized event. It took her a long time to respect herself for her achievement. The narrative she constructed leading up to the Olympics was "anything less than gold is a failure."

Think about that. This person was the second best in the *entire* world at her event, but because she wasn't number one, she perceived herself as a failure.

Sometimes you can place the bar too high for you to respect yourself. If you set the bar so high that you won't respect yourself until you win an Oscar, you will spend most, if not all, of your life not respecting yourself.

This is called result orientation, where you build the narrative of yourself around what you will accomplish. Although this type of narrative can be highly motivating, it can also crush you. Being obsessed with the outcome, you spend most of your preparation not enjoying the process. People who have this respect structure have a difficult time dealing with failure. Losing their will to compete. Many child prodigies fall into this category. That being said, most hyper-successful individuals have a result-oriented mindset.

Another type of narrative is process orientation where you feel fulfilled when you are engaged in the process of getting better. This mindset handles losses better and enjoys preparation. These individuals, however, may feel unearned contentment since they forget that results are always part of the end game.

The idea is to integrate both orientations by utilizing process orientation during growth periods and result orientation while preparing for events. It can be beneficial to even oscillate between the two based on the emotional state you find yourself in.

The Power Bible

If you're overwhelmed with anxiety for an upcoming event, switch to a process orientation. Focusing on your actions and habits more than winning. If you're in a period of growth but feel you have plateaued, find a bigger stage for you to compete so you can focus on a more substantial goal. Over time you will cultivate the wisdom of knowing the appropriate mindset and values that will carry you to your goals.

Brendon: That was even discovered by Nazi concentration camp survivor, Viktor Frankl, in his book Man's Search for Meaning. He called it "Logotherapy," and it's something you should apply to your own life. This is really a foundational concept of personal frame.

How you explain the world to yourself, how you explain your narrative to yourself, and how your narrative in the world exists with other narratives will make or break your experience of life. How you hit your goals, where you end up, how you interact with others, and the value that you experience in your day-to-day activities will all suffer if you don't get it right.

If you get it wrong, you leave it open for other people to define your narrative for you, and they will do so in *their* best interest.

William: The final and most important tenet of cultivating self-respect is honesty. I used to be a pathological liar and this was, in part, due to having a very low self-esteem. My dad said, "When you lie to someone, you're telling yourself that they are more important than you." Meaning that in the subtext of every lie is the internal narrative that "who I am is not good enough, so I must lie."

Being a pathological liar was bad for my self-esteem. The worse I felt about myself, the more compulsive the lies. To cure myself, I first had to stop lying, go back and tell everyone the lies I had told them, and finally start the healing process.

Remember the adage, honesty is powerful, but complete transparency is foolish—they differ only in a matter of degree. Honesty is communicating an appropriate amount of information at the right time; transparency is releasing all relevant details with no strategic discretion.

The Power Bible

Being honest with others allows you to trust yourself. You are able to speak with more conviction. Being honest when it's difficult will make you respect yourself even more.

Trust has two components, honesty and reliability. If we have a friend who always tells the truth but is always late, we tend not to trust that they are going to live up to their word, even though they are honest about their past. This is because trust deals with both facts and future expectations.

The same goes for us as individuals. Even if we are honest with people, we can lose respect for ourselves if we do not do what we tell ourselves we are going to do. Failure to live up to the character that you have picked for yourself means that you won't trust yourself when you speak about your goals for that character.

Just because you are honest about the past doesn't mean you will tell the truth about the future. A person who does what they say they will do becomes clairvoyant, while a person who doesn't, becomes a liar. As Heraclitus wrote, "Character is destiny."

Brendon: The kind of honesty that we are challenging you to encourage in yourself is one of non-judgemental, straightforward, scientific observation. When being honest, don't be angry, emotional, or fearful. Instead, challenge yourself to be objective and straightforward.

I'm shorter than 6 foot. I'm 5 foot 9, or maybe 5 foot 10 if I wear the right shoes. I know that that's detrimental to me sometimes. When it comes to online dating, there are a lot of women who will put on their profiles "6 foot or shorter need not apply." That means that on its face, there are a lot of women who just don't want to talk to me because I'm not tall enough. Now, I can either accept that non-judgmentally and just go, "Well, that means I need to concentrate on women who aren't doing that." Or, I can try to argue with it in my mind, refuse to accept it, feel bad about being something that I can't change about myself, and somehow find a way to digest it. Everything but the first option is the less productive way to live because I'm refusing to accept a narrative that is factually true.

The Power Bible

Because of my height, I'm never going to be naturally as good at playing basketball as taller men, but that can either discourage me or can encourage me. If I'm dedicated to trying to play in the N.B.A., then that means I will have to change my plan in order to succeed. That's ok. Reality informs the way that I should plan my time and interact with the future to gain and achieve my goal, but arguing with it and not accepting it will never allow me to make the best possible decisions.

Respect Rituals

- The longer you lay in bed the more anxiety you have, the slower you move throughout the day. So in order to build daily respect, it's important that when you wake up you get out of bed as soon as possible. This is more important than waking up early. Keep track of whether you got out of bed quickly on a calendar, try and maintain a streak.
- On days where you feel sluggish and fall into self-attack, taking a cold shower or going for a run will both dispel anxiety and are easy ways to turn around a day.
- Outline your current character. Be ruthlessly honest with your assessment. Record rather than write your answer as many people will stop short of their self-assessment out of laziness. Ask yourself

  "How do I act against my own self-interest?"
  "What do I regularly that makes me lose respect for myself?"
  "What small things could I do that would make a big difference in my life?"
  "What do I respect about myself?"
  "What don't I respect about myself?"

  These questions are just a launching pad. Talk until you have nothing left to say. Do this practice every couple of months and keep track of how you have grown.
- Ask yourself on a scale of 1-10 how much authority you have over yourself? What is one thing that you could do everyday that would increase that number?

- Ask yourself "how do the foods that I eat impact my respect?" Think about what kind of meals make you feel worse about yourself and what meals make you proud.
- Imagine that you're a character in a story. You're you, but the best version of yourself within your own story. Take a moment and think, what does your character desire out of life. What are his or her goals? Where would that character need to live to accomplish this goal? What is standing in the way? What excuses does he or she not accept? What does this character look like? What does this character do on a daily basis? What kind of food does he or she eat? What does this character do on weekends? How does he or she waste time?

2 - Acceptance

William: Acceptance, or self-acceptance, exists on a spectrum. On one extreme is a person who finds themselves so unacceptable that they can't take living with themselves anymore, and commits suicide. At the other extreme is a person who accepts themselves so much that they have no problem demanding what they want from life.

Most of us fall somewhere in the middle, but even our level of self-acceptance varies based on the context. For example, if you are interacting with a person you perceive is higher status than you, then you will tend to accept yourself less.

Accepting yourself is a misnomer. We are instructed by advertising and our social environment to find parts of ourselves unacceptable. We break ourselves down piece by piece and measure ourselves against an impossible standard. As a result, most people don't accept parts of themselves.

Before going any further I want to clarify the difference between self-acceptance and self-respect. A person who respects themselves feels no general anxiety when they are alone. A person who completely accepts themselves feels no social anxiety. Self-acceptance is your projection of people's perception of you. Respect is your perception of yourself.

The Power Bible

The more you accept yourself the easier it will be to do things that will make you respect yourself. The more you respect yourself the easier it will be for you to believe people will accept you. People profit from you finding yourself unacceptable. Corporations sell you the "cure" for your unacceptability, but what they are selling is a distraction. You put on a new shirt and accept yourself the first few times you wear it, but over time that shirt becomes ordinary and you go back to feeling unacceptable.

This feeling of unacceptability is validated by our interactions with the world. A few examples include: You not being qualified to work most jobs; you being an unacceptable romantic partner to most of the world's population, and your parents finding parts of your life unacceptable. That's right, even your genetically linked parents disapprove of some aspect of your life. So, why should you accept yourself?

There are two reasons. First, the better you get at accepting yourself the more people will accept you. Second, other people's acceptance is unstable, so why base your ability to accept yourself on it?

The requirements that people have on the company they keep are not as rigid as they say. There are companies that swore they would never have a black employee a hundred years ago who now have a black CEO. There are women who have said they would never date a guy under 6'2" who are happily married to a man who's 5'7". There are parents who said they would disown their child if they ever caught him smoking pot, who now brag about their son's marijuana business in California.

Most people's "standards" or "requirements' are empty phrases made to fill the silence and make them sound more discriminating than they are to cultivate an image of a respectable individual. More importantly, the more parts of yourself that you accept without question, the more easily others will accept you.

The self-acceptance spectrum is a helpful model because there isn't a particular moment that we do accept ourselves. Self-acceptance is both continuous and situational. You can tell how much you have accepted yourself by how much social pressure you are able to withstand without going into self-attack or changing your behavior.

Social pressure can make you disavow something that you've accepted about yourself for a long time, but after someone says a negative thing about it, you create a complex for yourself. I remember a girl in college who told me, "Will, you're just a little too short." I'm 5'9" and have always been happy with my height, until that moment. Her casual statement made the rest of the world grow several inches. This contributed to the noise in my head. I caught myself deferring to taller people in conversation. Using it as a way to explain away their success with girls and never allowing myself to take responsibility for my failures.

The noise in your head I mentioned earlier are the anxieties you have around your insecurities. The bigger the stage, the louder they scream. The noise is the persistent hum at the back of your mind. There is nothing more parasitic to your frame than a lack of self-acceptance.

A lot of people state that they don't accept themselves in order to maintain a growth mindset. Their philosophy goes something like, "I don't accept myself because I could always be better." I somewhat support this mentality. Mainly because it's difficult to get enough leverage over yourself to improve when you are completely content with who you are in any particular moment. But as with most things, the way you do this matters.

There are, for better or for worse, immutable facts about ourselves— things that will never change. Then there are things that we can change and improve. The immutable characteristics include things like race, skin tone, height, face structure, place of origin, etc. Rather than hide them, we need to ritualistically construct a narrative of pride around those features.

My internal narrative ritual occurs every morning. I stand in front of the mirror naked and I go through each part of my body and I say, "I love and accept this part of myself."

We experience ourselves in parts. For example, we might like our nose, but not like our eyes, we might like our calves but not like our neck. This lack of acceptance of certain parts of ourselves keeps us from accepting ourselves in entirety.

The more you do this exercise, the more you will believe what you're saying. Since most things that we value are subjective, all we have to do is take the time to appreciate our features rather than critique them. With repetition, the narrative of appreciation will become stronger and the critical narrative will be weaker. It helps if you attach reasons why you like that part of yourself. Humans love logical explanations so if you can construct logical reasons on why you like your "deficiencies" you will be able to accept them faster. The more emotion you put into telling yourself this, the more powerful the effects.

Brendon: It's weird, but Bill does it and it works.

Honestly, some of the activities, rituals, and exercises that we're going to describe, especially ones that have to do with your own personal frame, are going to sound strange and different. They're going to make you feel slightly uncomfortable. But the truth is that if you don't want to receive the same results you've been receiving your whole life, you're going to have to try new things and those things are going to feel uncomfortable at first.

A phrase I'm fond of is "Ordinary actions for ordinary results, extraordinary actions for extraordinary results."

William: The reason why you might feel uncomfortable is that at first, saying you accept those parts of yourself will feel like a lie. You have so deeply bought into the story of your inferiority that you are unable to compliment yourself without feeling like you are lying.

As we mentioned before, lying attacks our self-esteem. That being said, this is an instance where you should say something that makes you feel dishonest. This is because your feeling that these characteristics make you deficient is a lie, and you are going through the process of accepting the truth, which is that you should be proud of your immutable characteristics.

The Power Bible

I'm half Indian, half Black and was brought up in Indian culture where dark skin isn't attractive and I had family members who would say things like "you would be so attractive if you weren't so dark." Statements like these got deep into my subconscious. When I got older I blamed my lack of romantic success on my skin color.

The reason why I was not experiencing success was because of my lack of self-acceptance. I behaved in ways that sabotaged my efforts. I protected the belief that I was unacceptable with actions that would assure it would remain the case.

Brendon: Notice, the people who might have rejected Bill previously for his skin tone might still reject him, but there's a whole audience of people who accept him because of his skin tone that he was not exposing himself to because he had bad self-belief and low self-value.

Many people with bad personal frames are trapped trying to win over an audience that rejected them, rather than accepting themselves and finding the audience that would love them authentically. When Bill changed his personal frame, he was able to find those people who overwhelmingly accepted him because of his skin tone.

Previously, the ability to even notice people who accepted him was impossible. The personal frame of low self-worth prevents one from picking up the social signals that others, who have high self-value, notice all the time. The personal frame that doesn't work is one of "I have to be good enough." Having this frame places someone in a "not good enough" place *to begin with*. If Bill doesn't feel "good enough," he's going to seek people who also feel that way so he can win them over, thereby discharging the tension created by his personal frame. However, that will never happen, or at least the likelihood of it won't happen, so long as he's continually looking for people to win over. Ultimately, his skin tone isn't really the reason he's "finding" people who are rejecting him.

William: I realized my skin tone was never the reason. I was just a weird dude with mediocre social skills and bad fashion. I blamed my race because it was a convenient way for me not to take responsibility for growing as a person and investigating my blind spots.

The Power Bible

Remember this: if people don't like you, that's your problem. It's not their problem and a lot of times we project our baggage onto other people to avoid growing.

Brendon: And when you externalise the problem rather than internalize, you remove it from your locus of control, and that sends a covert message to you that you don't control your world and can't change your life. Believing that your problems and their solutions are *outside of you* prevents you from seeing solutions that you can provide.

This mindset prevents you from actually achieving the things that you want to achieve. The more you believe that you have the power to control good or bad outcomes, the more likely it is that you will actually achieve those outcomes.

Acceptance Rituals

- The degree to which you will accept yourself will change drastically based on the social context you find yourself in. Ask yourself in varying moments of the day "On a scale of 1-10 how much do I accept myself right now?" Ask yourself "What would I do if I accepted myself a little bit more than I do?" After you give yourself an answer, go do that thing.
- Pull out the recorder and ask yourself what physical features of yours do you find unacceptable or that you think that other people don't accept. After you get the answer, distinguish whether these features are immutable or mutable.
- For immutable features that you find unacceptable, come up with a narrative of how these features are a strength, then whenever you feel self-conscious about this, use that narrative to quiet your mind. Say this narrative daily in front of the mirror for maximum effect. The more regularly you do this, the more rapid an identity level change will take place.
- Ask yourself in what situations do you find yourself feeling the most unacceptable? Why?
- Know that many of us protect ourselves from feeling inferior by feigning disinterest. Stating that going to such events/clubs are beneath you. Ask yourself what events, clubs, and jobs do you

not attend because you are afraid they won't accept you? Make an effort to start going to these events. If you are not accepted, run a diagnostic as to why; don't allow yourself to use any excuses that involves an immutable trait.

3 - Conditioning

William: Conditioning is the process of training a person to behave in a certain way or to accept certain circumstances. Everything we know about the world is the result of our conditioning. You were conditioned to accept that your name is your name, your parents are your parents, and the words you're reading have meaning.

Much of our conditioning falls under the umbrella of social conditioning. Social conditioning is necessary for society to function. Almost all our customs, behaviors, desires and values come from our interactions with others. Our ability to learn via social conditioning is how civilization came into existence.

That being said, all of your insecurities are a result of your conditioning. Once again, there are great things that come from conditioning, like the instinctive response to stop a child from running with scissors, to provide assistance to someone who is hurt, that killing without reason or authority is bad. These are all conditioned concepts that benefit society as a whole. But what is great for the collective often limits the individual. On top of that, many socially conditioned narratives are just wrong or interpreted incorrectly by the masses.

Part of the reason for this is that there is money to be made off of people's need to belong. The more inferior you feel, the more likely you are to spend money on products to alleviate that pain. That is why billions of dollars are spent on advertising. Advertising works on the premise that there is something you lack, and what you lack is keeping you from being accepted, but if you purchase their product, this will no longer be a problem.

If you buy into this cultural framing, you will end up judging yourself hyper-critically. You assume that people see your worst features rather than your best. A few years ago, there was a Dove brand soap commercial where a person described himself and then another person who just talked to him for 30 seconds in the waiting room would describe that person to a police sketch artist. The drawings were massively different. As the subject focuses only on their flaws, whereas the person who met them in the hallway focused on what they actually looked like. It's funny that other people can have a lot better perception of what you look like than you do.

Brendon: I love that example.

William: Self-attack comes from us not meeting the values of society. This happens through passive brainwashing. For example, in Indian culture, it is bad to have dark skin, while in Scandinavian culture, being pale is looked at as a non-ideal.

Passive brainwashing is where you go through your social environment like a sponge, taking in whatever the media is selling. You need a nice car! You need a hot girlfriend/boyfriend! You need to have an Ivy League degree! Tons of money! If you don't have these things you're not valuable and if you come in contact with people who have these things, you need to defer to them.

What we encourage in this book is manual brainwashing or auto-suggestion. This is where you actively choose the information that you're interacting with selectively. Then once you pick a source you listen to it everyday, multiple times a day, for years.

Over time, the information that you're interacting with becomes part of you. The reason we suggest this level of repetition is that in moments of high stress you tend to fall back onto socially conditioned narratives. The longer you listen to something, the more it controls your decision-making process. Think about this, you have to see an ad seven times on average before you're compelled to take action. So we want you to advertise good ideals and principles so that you make a decision in accordance with those values.

The Power Bible

One product that has transformed my life is Jocko Willink, Discipline Equals Freedom Field Manual. Jocko Willink is a former Navy SEAL and he has a compilation of short essays that I listen to get access to the mindset of a Navy SEAL Commander. A Navy SEAL's ability to keep a strong inner frame in high-pressure situations is what keeps them alive.

So, in a sense, whenever I listen to Jocko, I lessen the power that the mainstream media has over my decision-making faculties and I strengthen my own. The most terrifying and awesome part of auto-suggestion is the degree to which it will control your actions. Listening to Jocko for a couple of hours a day for several months, it's now impossible for me to hit the snooze button. I feel the compulsion to strive to become the strongest version of myself, to go to the gym multiple times a day, to reach out to the people I love, to assert control over the mind.

Free will is an illusion; the reality is that our decisions are highly contingent on context and how we have been conditioned. So controlling your conditioning makes it easier to control your actions.

A question I get a lot is "Can I just read instead of listening?" My answer is that reading is not as effective as listening. That's because, with regard to the human species, reading is a new invention, it's only been around for around 5000 years. There's a good chance that your great grandparents didn't know how to read.

Whereas we have listened to audio commands since the dawn of our species. So, what is said resonates with us on a deeper level. Think about troops preparing for bootcamp. They are not handed a book with drills for them to carry out. They are screamed at day and night so that they reflexively listen to commands.

People in the self-help realm tend to read & listen to lots of different content. We advocate listening *to the same content* over and over and over again because it becomes reflexive in the way you think. The more you listen to the same message over and over again, the deeper in your subconscious it goes. The actor Anthony Hopkins reads each of his scripts over a hundred times so that he can fully internalize the character he's going to portray. So listen and read to the same fulfilling content thousands of times so that you become the character you want to play.

Brendon: It's not about novelty, it's about repetition. As we've already said, humans lived for thousands and thousands of years in an ancient setting, and as animals, millions of years in groups that did not have writing, where people were not as alone as they are today. This is the only time in history that humans have had to contend with an environment rich in messages, constant, streaming, faster-than-we-can-process messages. It's also the only time that those messages have been *against* your self-interest. In the primordial past, you would've been surrounded by positive and encouraging messages most of the time because your success was the group's success. It was against others' self-interest to give you messages that questioned your ability to contribute. However, now that's not the case.

This is important to understand because you unconsciously pick up the values of the people and groups around you, which is why the people who are most successful surround themselves with the best people and are very careful about who they allow into their life. They're also careful about the narratives that they allow into their life.

So, avoiding things that disconfirm the positive beliefs you have about yourself and the world around you is actually essential to try to build a very strong foundational personal frame. It's also important to challenge your personal frame by testing it, but this is different than internalizing messages about it *not being enough*.

William: We've all heard that quote, 'you are the average of the five people you hang out with most" but nobody explains why. Whenever you're relating with somebody, you're building a bridge of communication between them. The more you relate with that person, the stronger the bridge gets.

But here's the thing about a bridge: stuff crosses from both ends. When you build a bridge, you get both the good habits from the person and the bad habits as well. Nietzsche wrote, "Whoever fights with monsters should see to it that he does not become a monster in the process. For when you gaze long into an abyss, the abyss also gazes into you."

As vigilant as you can be, you are going to be in their frame from time to time when communicating with them. This means that for moments in conversation you will experience the world through their point of view.

This is the benefit of hiring a coach and being in their presence, rather than just reading their book. You tend to hold yourself to the standard of the people you are around.

Brendon: This is why self-brainwashing, known as autosuggestion, is so important for someone who's trying to change their life. You're limited by the experiences you've had, and if you're looking to break through limitations you must break patterns that have potentially been running for years.

Even if your life is "uncomfortable," you're used to it, and deep down your brain & body know they can survive in that environment because they *have* been surviving.

If that's the case, then when you attempt to change your life, even for the better, you're going to experience a lot of fear and new emotions that are very scary. Those could be fear of failure, fear of success, many different fears. The thing that's going to carry you through that fear and cause you to continue to act is your ability to self-brainwash and autosuggest to create the reality you want.

That's *faith*, and acting in the face of that fear is going to require a deep belief in your unconscious mind that you can handle whatever is coming. That requires a shift, and autosuggestion is a good way to internalize those messages. Those thoughts manifest themselves in your life, not as "the secret" or some supernatural way, but because they will help guide your brain to notice information it would've normally avoided or discarded.

William: Exactly. James Allen wrote in '*As A Man Thinketh*': "A **man** is literally what he **thinks**, his character being the complete sum of all his thoughts." And "It's not the circumstances that make the man, they reveal him to himself." And a lot of what allows us to withstand those

The Power Bible

moments are simple quotes like "To be the man you gotta be the man.," or "The difficult we do immediately, the impossible takes a little longer."

The real power of autosuggestion is that a lot of our parents, even though they tried their best, left holes in our value set. But by utilizing auto-suggestion, we can be our own parent and instill the values we wish we were taught as a child

The younger you are when you adopt a belief the harder it is to rewrite. This is why inferiority complexes are so difficult to overcome. Whether it's your race, gender, class, or height, society's default message of the role that you're supposed to play will limit you.

There are a lot of narratives that aren't easily available. Meaning that you can get past these things but you need to believe that they're not limiting factors, you need to believe that your race, your height, your gender isn't limiting your success *but actually is the reason why you will be successful.*

Now it's important to remember that we are all, to some degree, ok with these traits, but what you must be aware of is that the more social pressure there is in a situation, the more likely you are to feel insecure.

One of my smart friends had a 4.0 GPA but when he took the LSAT, he was caught up with how quickly the white people in the room - he was black - were filling out their names and that got him in his head for the entire test. Now his thoughts didn't manifest as "I feel inferior because I am black" but the fact of the matter is in a high-pressure environment, the thought surfaced "oh, they're filling up their bubbles on their names so much faster than me, it must mean that I'm not as smart as them," which caused him to score way below what he was scoring on his practice test.

This has also been shown in studies where people put down that they're of African-American descent before they take the GRE, they score on average 50 points lower than if they were to have gone in without putting down their race beforehand.

Brendon: All our stories come from the past *necessarily*, and the past was one way and the present, which is really only continuing to move into the future, is whatever we decide we want it to be. The future is truly yet to be determined. It's true that it's influenced by the past, but it isn't *determined*. The mistake many people tend to make is to assume that their present circumstances, which *are* determined by the past, will be their future circumstances, which *are not* determined by the past.

In fact, the future is determined by *the present*. This is an important metaphysical truth: although the present is in fact unchangeable, the future is absolutely changeable and *you have the power to change it through decision making and action*.

It's the direction you decide to move and how much influence you exert over your own experience in the present that will eventually determine the future. Keep in mind that you will have a future self. That self is someone you will eventually become, and their circumstances will eventually be your circumstances. The actions you take in the present will influence the character and nature of that future self.

If you believe that things in the past or even in the present will affect the outcome of the future *outside* of you taking action then you are forfeiting your authority over your own life. A strong frame is like a bulwark against any narrative, past or present, internal or social, that seeks to undermine the authority you have in determining your own future or acting with powerful action in the present.

William: The easier you are to offend the weaker your frame. The stronger your frame the more difficult it is to make you upset. You will notice that the stronger your frame gets, the harder it will be to interpret something as an insult. The highest of this is to interpret every person's action or non-action as a compliment, but we'll get to that later.

I cannot recommend enough, checking out Jocko Willink's, *Discipline Equals Freedom Field Manual*.

Conditioning Rituals

- We are conditioned by what we watch and listen. The first step of getting control of your conditioning is to ask yourself on a regular basis "What am I passively conditioning myself with?"

- In response to your answer to the first question ask yourself "What emotions and beliefs does (blank) give me?" What is a better source for me to listen to?
- Listen to your source material multiple times a day. An easy way to remember is if you think "Should I listen to it right now?" Do it. We suggest Jocko's Field Manual, but there are other sources. Listening repeatedly to motivational material, our audiobook, etc. will work.
- Ask yourself "Who has conditioned me?" What are some of the good things that they have conditioned into you? What are some of the bad things? Who has conditioned you will have an answer that will change often, so ask yourself this question regularly.

4 - Outcome Independence

William: Outcome independence is the mindset of going into a situation and not needing a particular outcome. It is difficult to master but if you can learn the art of giving all of your intent but being free from the outcome, you will find that you will have the ability to be very creative and productive, and with no anxiety.

Outcome independence is important in developing a strong frame because it allows you to keep a light-hearted disposition. This will help you keep your wits when someone disagrees with you. It also will aid you in negotiations because the person who has the advantage is the one who cares the least about the outcome. That's why it's easy for a billionaire to have a strong frame because they need less from you than you need from them.

Brendon: What's important to understand is that outcome independence means acting for the pleasure of the action, having observance of the outcome, and having intentions for a good outcome, but not having any attachments to the outcome.

So, what does this mean? This is what someone might describe as acting with detachment, even stoic detachment. It means accepting that I can't control the outcome, the only thing I can control is how good I play the game and whether or not I play the game well enough to get the outcomes I desire.

I remind myself that whatever action I'm taking is just a big experiment and really, everything is just practice for another scenario where I will succeed in the future. If you remove the need for the action that you're taking to have a specific outcome right at the moment, you free yourself from the emotions that will force you to try to control it and usually ruin it by trying to control it. I sometimes even remind myself of these things in writing because I carry a small notebook on me.

William: Absolute control is an illusion; an unachievable standard.

Brendon: The best analogy I can think of is from wrestling. I wrestled in high school, I did mixed martial arts just after college and in college and I had cage fights. I have an undefeated M.M.A. record. And one of the sure-fire ways to lose a wrestling match is by walking into the match with the idea that you are going just to force your opponent to the ground.

This is foolish because they have plans that are different from yours, and as soon as your plans start going wrong, you have nothing to fall back on. It's just like Mike Tyson says, "everyone has a plan until they get punched in the face."

You have to be able to flexibly move with the situation and being able to move with it, staying with an intention in mind but not forcing something to be a certain kind of way, will allow you to be flexible enough to actually achieve the outcomes you're looking for because the situation changes from moment to moment; either in a wrestling match or in life.

Just like this, plans in your life to achieve your goals must shift and move with changing circumstances. Act *as if* you'll achieve the outcome, act with full confidence, but be open to other things happening and roll with those new challenges and circumstances. Being too tied to an outcome will prevent you from taking the risks that might be necessary to achieve it.

William: The opposing fighter has a competing frame, and only one of your frames will win. Now if your frame is that you are going to demolish your opponent, as soon as you get evidence that contradicts that frame, like getting punched several times in the face or getting knocked down, it will be hard to keep your frame, which might lead to you losing the fight.

Brendon: The same is true for stand-up comedy. Stand-up Comedy is a frame battle with the audience, and it's not just a frame battle with one member of the audience, it's a frame battle with *all* members of the audience. And they have different frames, competing frames sometimes, and you have a microphone and the spotlight is on you.

If you are trying to stick to your pre-written jokes and material, you won't be flexible enough to move with the feelings of the audience and you'll end up losing them and bombing.

Comedians need to have a plan, they have to know where they're going but they have to be nimble enough to work with the feelings and the judgments and the values and desires of the audience to guide them to where the comedian wants them to go.

William: One of the issues that I had in stand-up was that I started taking being funny too seriously. I stopped having fun on stage because I *needed* the laughter to feel good. I needed the audience to find me funny and that was a form of outcome-dependence. My behavior on stage communicated that I was stressed, and because the audience empathizes with the speaker, they felt stressed watching my performance, which made them too uncomfortable to laugh.

Whenever you need a particular outcome, it makes it almost impossible to have fun because fun requires you to be in the moment. You cannot have fun while worrying and if you need a particular outcome you will worry.

Worrying about the outcome turns everything into a finite game. Ideally, you'll want to be playing an infinite game. A finite game is played for the purpose of winning; an infinite game is played for the purpose of continuing play.

Your life is an infinite game, and the finite games you feel you must win are illusions. The only goal is to continue to play. Remember that if you feel like you must play you cannot be playful.

Outcome independence is necessary to make the decisions to live the life that you want. To pursue your dreams you must deal with the reality that you might try your hardest and still fail. Now there are those who need to succeed and that's what drives them, but the problem with this is when things are not working. They end up making decisions that could have a negative effect on their career or life in the long term out of desperation.

The amount of skin in the game you have might cause you to stop thinking rationally. An extreme example of this is where someone loses a lot of money gambling and keeps doubling down because they need to win again. An element from my own life was when I was trading currencies and I had too much money in the market to follow my principles which ended up making me lose a lot of money.

Like self-acceptance, self-respect, self-conditioning, the degree to which you are free from the outcome is on a spectrum. The more invested you are in a project or goal, the harder it will be to remain outcome independent. You can tell if you have too much dependence on the outcome if you start to suffer from anxiety, panic attacks, and paranoia.

In these situations, it might be impossible to convince yourself that you do not care about the outcome. If paranoia or panic attacks start to become the norm, figure out how you can split the responsibilities to mitigate the stress of the upcoming event.

A person who can turn life into an infinite game will be able to keep level during times of great uncertainty. An element of confidence is your ability to remain certain that you will be able to persevere in uncertain situations.

Outcome Independence Rituals

- What is a place that you do not have freedom from the outcome? Why is this part of your life so important to you? What are ways that you could mitigate this need for control?
- Identify the relationships where you are playing a finite game. Meaning, what situations or relationships that you focused on winning. How is that limiting you?

5 - Context

William: A frame is the context or belief through which a person, situation, or a conversation is perceived.

Frame control is a foundational concept in this book. The four other pillars of inner frame are inward facing. Dealing with how you perceive yourself. Context deals with how you interpret what you perceive.

The two default context we have when interpreting what we perceive are the victim and champion frame. The victim frame corrupts information while the champion frame builds. What I mean by "the victim frame corrupts" is that it reads powerlessness into any situation. If you have a strong victim frame it will be impossible for you to feel in control of your life. It takes information that might be positive and corrupts it into something harmful.

An example, you are highly qualified for a job, the first stage of the interview process is a group interview, they talk to you at the beginning but then focus on the other candidates. The other candidates are the opposite gender, you take this to mean that they are simply not interested in your gender at this office and begin to get offended.

It turns out that the reason they didn't spend much time talking to you is because they were already impressed with your resume and didn't have to talk to you for a long time before concluding that you should go to the next round.

The insidious nature of the victim frame is that it leads to habitual self-sabotage. In the example above you might start acting dismissively towards them because you were offended which ends up with them choosing someone else for the job

Brendon: The difference between victim frame and champion frame comes down to just two sides of a point of view. The victim frame is one in which the subject, you, feels like the world is acting *upon you* and there's nothing you can do about it. And the champion frame is the one in which you feel you are acting *upon the world* and the changes you make in it are meaningful.

William: Champion frame differs from the victim frame in that a victim's frame is pessimistic and blameless, while a champion's frame is optimistic and responsible. The champion interprets events in the world as if the world were conspiring to help them accomplish their goal. While also believing that they are responsible for what happens in their life, good or bad.

That means a champion is not likely to arrive at the conclusion that the world is at fault for their problems. A champion believes that they are responsible for creating solutions for their problems. They also believe they have the power and ability to do so.

Brendon: Context is a huge part of the inner frame because the way that you explain the thoughts that you have or the situations that you end up in to yourself will encourage or deteriorate your inner frame.

A champion sees evidence from the world that challenges their frame as an opportunity to overcome, to rise to the occasion, to act and therefore strengthen their frame. Champions act in a way that, even in defeat, reinforces their belief that *they* have a say as to what the outcome will be. Ultimately, acting this way, even if one doesn't succeed, encourages one's self-belief and adds to an already strong frame.

Having a champion mentality is foundational to success; otherwise, challenging circumstances will overwhelm and disintegrate your frame.

A champion fighter once lost a match to an opponent he expected to defeat. After losing, *he held his champion frame* by believing and understanding that it was *he* who *lost* the fight, not the opponent who *won* it. This is important to understand, as this small mental maneuver maintained his mastery over what happened. This is called taking responsibility.

The fighter trained for the next fight, accepting responsibility for *his* loss by continuing to train and overcoming the weaknesses that had led to him losing the previous fight. When the rematch came around, he won.

William: Much like self-acceptance, the victim and champion frames are on a spectrum and situational. There are places where you will be more prone to feeling like a victim. There are places where it will be easy for you to feel like a champion.

Places where it is easy for you to feel like a victim are places where you have a low level of competence or places where you are heavily invested in the outcome. Places where you have low or no status or where your status in the environment is going down.

Places where it is easy for you to feel like a champion are areas where you have a high level of competence, situations where you are not heavily invested in the outcome, or where you have fixed or high status or where you are on the ascent.

Also, there are certain relationships where we are more prone to feeling like a victim or a champion. Relationships where you are not the dominant one will be easy for you to feel like a victim. For example, your boss is not likely to feel like a victim when around you but it's easy for you to feel like a victim around your boss.

This is because on some level you feel as if they have control over your life. The reason I use the word "feel" is because power imbalances exist in casual relationships as well, but we still feel victimized even if on-paper the person has no control over our lives.

A litmus test for how deep you are in victim frame is to notice how often you complain about a certain relationship in your life. If you find yourself complaining a lot about particular relationship, you are deep in victim frame in that relationship.

The frightening and exciting thing about these two frames is that they become more powerful the more you feed them. The more you search for how you are a victim, in a circumstance or in a relationship, the more likely you will do it in other relationships and circumstances.

For oppressed members of society since the narrative of victimhood is pushed by the media which makes it easier for you to assume that your gender or race is the cause of your problems, even if this is true, conditioning yourself to believe that you are a victim is violent towards your self esteem and will have you reach incorrect inferences when interpreting people's behavior towards you.

Having a victim frame can make it easier for you to being coerced to act violently. For example, most school shooters have a manifesto where they talk or write about being a victim their entire life. What white supremacist and Islamic radicalists have in common is that they believe that the entire world is against them. Some members of the group feel so victimized by the world that they carry out violent acts on others. Hitler used a narrative about how the German people were victims to grab power in Germany validate his reasons for declaring war against the world.

The victim frame taken to its conclusion ends in the suffering of the people around you. It gets rid of positive emotions with ruthless efficiency and replaces them with negative ones.

Developing a champion frame is simple. Interpret everything that people do or say to you as a compliment. Interpret your doubts as a symptom of not working hard enough or a sign that you need to find mentors or books to help you find a way. Finally, laugh off failures while taking aggressive action to ensure that mistakes will never happen again.

If you can make yourself laugh on demand by framing your development you have what we call a dynamic frame.

Champion and victim frames are how you interpret events that happen in your life or out in the world. Dynamic and rigid frames are measurements of how malleable your worldview is.

A dynamic frame is a frame that integrates new information and evolves over time. The American Legal System is an example of a dynamic frame. There are new laws being drafted, new interpretations of old laws, and the removal of antiquated laws. A rigid frame is more akin to the 10 Commandments. Simple, clear but lacks nuance and does not adapt with the times.

People with dynamic frames are better equipped to integrate new information into their frame than people with rigid frames. This is because contradictory information doesn't destroy dynamic frames but it does destroy rigid frames.

Dynamic frames allow for nuance and uncertainty, rigid frames are meant to be all-encompassing so there is no room for new information that doesn't fit within their preexisting paradigm. An example of a group that has a rigid frame are religious fundamentalists, meaning someone who believes that there are no truths that exist outside of their religious canon.

This person might speak with certainty and exhibit a lot of the traits of having a strong frame, but their frame limits how they can meaningfully interact with the world. There are fundamentalist groups who refuse to use modern technology and give women rights because that would challenge the validity of their religious text.

People with dynamic frames, on the other hand, will have weaker frames early on. Not relying on an all-encompassing model for what you think and believe will create scenarios where you are unsure about what to do. Existential dread is a byproduct of having a dynamic frame because you are aware of the limitless possibilities and the validity of varying points of view. Over time with diligent thought, humor about insecurities and constant action, the person with dynamic frame becomes far more convincing than the person with a rigid frame as they are able to not only integrate new information but also make inferences that utilize different schools of thought.

The utilization of different paradigms help a person with a dynamic frame deal with trauma easier than those with a rigid frame. For example, if you believe that bad things don't happen to good people because God protects them, but you lose your child at a young age from a freak accident, you either have to accept that your child was a bad person or that your worldview is wrong.

If you accept that you might have been wrong about that part of your world view, then your whole world view might be wrong. This can cause you to have a meltdown, a crisis, as not only do you have to deal with the grief of a loss, but your concept of the world falling apart as well. The person who has a dynamic frame is used to their worldview being disconfirmed by new or contradictory information, so is able to rebound from a catastrophic event easier. People who tend to have a rigid frame are those who identify strongly with an ideology.

"To be an ideologue is to have all of the terrible things that are associated with religious certainty and none of the utility." - Jordan B. Peterson.

The final part of context and frame is understanding the implicit rules of the conversation and environment. Every conversation is a type of game. Much like many sports use a ball, but use the ball in different ways, the same is true with the words we use in conversation.

There are certain phrases permissible to say with friends but not co-workers. There are certain thoughts that should be expressed at work but not to your spouse. Context is even more nuanced as there are certain phrases you can say to your lover at night but not in the morning. Some things you can say to a friend one on one, but not in the company of others.

A person with a strong frame but unaware of the nuance of context will be denied opportunities they never knew were on the table. The better you get at understanding the rules of the game you're playing, and more specifically, which rules others think that exist but *you* know do not, the more efficiently you can socially strategize how you will achieve success. This will allow you to diagnose what you may have done wrong and correct in real time, or it will allow you to understand what the fallout might be for taking a particular risk and do it anyway because the juice is worth the squeeze.

Context Rituals

- Ask yourself throughout the day if your thoughts are out of a Victim frame or a Champion frame.
- When you are offended by what someone said or did to you, look for a way to turn that gesture into a compliment.
- Periodically pick moments from your past that you felt victimized and find a way to laugh about the situation. This is best to do with petty grudges you hold.
- In situations when you feel powerless, ask yourself how you are responsible.
- Write out a list of places where you might have a rigid frame. Deconstruct beliefs you hold to be true to add layers of nuance to your understanding. Then do the same with opposing belief structures.

Emotions

II. Introduction to Emotions

Emotions are an indication from the deep brain on what's happening. Emotions *are not you*. It is of the utmost importance that this is understood. There are people in terrifying situations when fear has gripped them deep down, and yet still act. There are people overcome with desire, love, and enthusiasm who yet can calculate the best actions to take to achieve a goal.

The understanding and identification of an emotion is the first step to removing it from having power over you. As is said, the first step in defeating a demon is naming it. Once you know its name, it is known to you.

Before the reader jumps to the conclusion that a study of emotions is a waste of time, remember that the bottom of every social hierarchy is littered with unfortunate people who have never developed a vocabulary to understand their own emotions. Although the reader may not associate with these kinds of people, the dilemma is the same: to rule one's own emotions rather than be ruled by them. It's not only the lowliest of society who's emotions can lead them to ruin, lest we forget that Troy was destroyed by one man's lust.; Bernie Madoff, and the people he took advantage of, also know these same emotions.

To achieve power, one must understand the negative and positive emotions that influence one's frame. One must understand what they are, why they are, and how to use them to one's advantage. There are more emotions than are named here, but many emotions are blends or versions of those presented here. This section will bring a basic vocabulary and understanding, tools the reader can use to unpack and understand their own emotions.

Negative Emotions

Negative Emotional States

Inferiority

William: Inferiority is feeling guilt for your presence. Inferiority will make you feel baseless anxiety, a persistent worry of offending others with your presence, and the assumption that no one likes you.

It's important to say here that the feeling of inferiority is closely linked to the feeling of shame.

Shame is the feeling that you have done something unacceptable or are someone that's unacceptable.

Brendon: If you notice that a lot of our descriptions around shame or inferiority sounds like not having a frame, that's because not having a frame puts you in an inferior position. However, what we're talking about is inferiority as a static feeling or state where your natural disposition is to feel inferior, your "default."

The kind of feeling of inferiority we're describing here might cause one to think "I don't belong here" when at a party, or "These people have done so many things, what have I done?" when meeting their peers entering college or a new job.

This type of inferiority runs as a kind of background noise in the back of the mind, coloring all experiences after one feels it.

William: This is the result of a myriad of socially conditioned narratives. This comes from the advertising industrial complex which creates a need for you to purchase a product by implying that who you are isn't enough.

It also brings about historical narratives of classism, racism, and sexism. They come from our childhood and our relationship with our family.

These three things come together to create our meta-framework on how the world operates and how we fit in it. These narratives create our image of what a perfectly acceptable person looks like. How we differ from this image is where our inferiority complex comes from.

Where I confronted the specter of my insecurity was in college. I attended Baylor University for undergrad. The school was in Texas, and so although it was diverse, there were still many students who were racists. To put this in perspective, when Obama was elected President, some students hung an Obama doll from a noose. Others changed their profile picture to the confederate flag. A symbol of racism.

One of the students I was friends with was a closet racist and sent me a Nazi video asking what I thought about the points. The video was a hate campaign and the premise of the video was that black people are subhuman, and the grander narrative was on how all races were inferior to whites.

The video's propaganda had a profound effect on me. It made me second-guess everything I knew to be true. Up until that time I had characterized myself as an intelligent person, but after watching that video, I was convinced that I had a low IQ.

The scary thing about this was that I had a lifetime of academic achievement that could have discounted that belief but since I had never been exposed to the ideas in the video, and I had a weak frame, I figured that there must have been some other explanation for my previous academic successes.

I also started deferring to my white friends when debating anything academic. What was even more startling was that I would begin to stutter when talking to whites. This stutter would miraculously vanish if I was around people of any other race.

This kept getting worse until I had a conversation with my dad about it and he said.

"Why are you giving these people's assertions any validity? Most people who make videos like that are just trying to cure their own feelings of inferiority."

Even after having this conversation with my dad, I still found myself falling into the same traps. That's because after I watched the video I looked for evidence to support the belief about my own inferiority.

So after talking with my Dad, I went through the process to find new evidence to invalidate my beliefs about being inferior. This process was difficult because I didn't know that's what I was doing so I would fall back into believing I was inferior. This is because what we believe is a habitual thought, so it is easy to mindlessly go back to our previous beliefs.

I had spent years looking for evidence that I was less intelligent than whites. I had started reflexively looking to discredit people who were not white but had achieved success in the world. So it was hard to create a new belief because when I would start looking for evidence I would immediately search for a way to discredit it.

How I overrode this was by looking for representations of African and Indian success. I marveled at both my mother and father's families and how all their siblings have master degrees and how my cousins are successful.

I policed my mind, whenever I noticed myself slipping into old thoughts of inferiority I would counter them with new information I had learned. Slowly over time, I let go of the identity that was addicted to feeling inferior and replaced it with an identity of someone who was proud of being who he was.

What I want you to take notice is that once I had made the decision to believe what they said in the video, I protected that belief by building a wall of evidence to support it, even if that meant limiting my own abilities to make sure that new belief stayed intact.

Brendon: This is such a good story because it shows two very powerful things. The first is that feelings of inferiority stemmed from a belief and the brain automatically – I mean automatically, it's important that the reader understands this — seeks to reinforce beliefs already held about the world.

So for some beliefs you hold, you yourself don't even understand that you have them. The brain creates beliefs based on life experience before you, the subject, even know that those beliefs are created. Experiences you have in your life cause a reaction in your brain, and beliefs are formed *before* you have any awareness of them. As a result, the emotions or feelings that you experience, from the inner workings of your deep brain, are many times a mystery to you and must be analyzed to be understood. This is why people have always gone to shamans, mystics, counselors and other professionals to talk through why they have the feelings they have and do the things they do. It's also why many people feel a longing to create art; to externalize the mysterious feelings inside them.

When we realize that we have inaccurate beliefs about the world, beliefs that don't correspond to reality, we have to actively remind ourselves again and again that those beliefs are wrong. We can do this by reminding ourselves about the evidence, finding examples of where those old beliefs are wrong. As an example, if you get passed over for a job, you can combat the belief of inferiority "I'm not a good candidate," by reminding yourself *why you are a good candidate*. Make a list.

Back to Bill's story, Bill had to *first* understand that he had created a new belief from watching that stupid video and *then* had to create a plan for going around finding disconfirming evidence to show that his belief that black people are inferior is actually wrong because there are plenty of examples of black people succeeding. So clearly that belief cannot be true in the world.

The second thing that's important to understand is that in a situation in which someone is seeking to create feelings of inferiority in you, they are doing so because they feel threatened by you and that only—you need to understand this—*confirms your superiority, power and status in relation to them.*

A champion would interpret someone else attempting to make them feel inferior as evidence that they are in fact powerful.

William: You have to be sensitive to the types of thoughts you have about yourself.

The Power Bible

It wasn't coming up consciously, "I am inferior because I am Black and Indian." Instead, it manifested in my assumptions about myself and other people; it *explained the world I observed to me.*

Feelings of inferiority are so crippling and hard to get over because we get addicted to the narratives we tell ourselves. I want you to think about your feelings of inferiority as a trance that you have put yourself under.

You hypnotized yourself into believing that you're not enough. Now you're trying to break out of the trance but it is difficult because you've spent years hypnotizing yourself to believe that others are better than you. You will have moments of clarity followed by days, weeks, years of being back in trance. The key is to know when you're back in the trance and wake yourself up.

There are two things you must do in tandem. You must develop pride for your immutable traits and improve your mutable traits. Your race, height, place of origin, face, and skin tone are all for the most part immutable. How much money you make, how in shape you are, how much you know, and how charismatic you are, are all things that are under your control.

If you've forgotten our techniques on how to accept yourself reread the inner-frame section on self-acceptance.

Brendon: Inferiority is so sinister and challenging to diagnose and move beyond because it restricts your view of the frame that you're holding when you're in that negative emotion. It restricts your view of the world and will prevent you from taking the actions necessary to overcome and get outside of it.

This is because the paradigm you're using to filter-in important information is being chosen from a frame of inferiority. The feeling of inferiority changes your mind to focus on survival, and survival is about staying small, staying safe, and *not changing anything.* If you have goals in your life, they're going to require change, both of yourself and of your environment. You'll have to make those changes, and if you're focused on survival you will not make them.

The Power Bible

The way to overcome feelings of inferiority is by deciding to have a new belief and investigating your own beliefs. Ask yourself, "Is this really true? Is this really a true thing about the world that I believe? What am I feeling inferior to and in relationship toward and can I investigate the truth of it?"

Every single person reading this book could run ten miles right now unless you are truly morbidly obese and can't get up and move around or have heart problems, every single person reading these words can get up and run 10 miles. The fact that you don't think you could is a limitation, and informed by your beliefs. Those beliefs would radically change if someone walked through your front door right now and put a gun to your head and said, "Hey, you start running and if you stop before you hit ten miles, I'm going to shoot you dead," almost everyone, nearly 100% of everyone reading this, aside from the people who truly, truly did not want to live, would all do it. And that's because you are restricting your beliefs from a feeling of inferiority unless of course, you're reading this book and already know you can run 10 miles, in which case you would just go do it.

William: What you have to be cognizant of when dealing with inferiority is that you will not let compliments land. If someone says "Wow, you're handsome" and you believe that you are ugly, you will explain away this compliment as them just being polite or worse, them mocking you.

You will find that when you feel inferior you will be easy to offend. So if you are in the habit of letting little things people say bother you for hours, this is a sign of feeling inferior because if you truly felt comfortable with your standing you would shrug off the statement.

Now a lot of people are good at mimicking the behavior of someone who is confident, but in this chapter, we're concerned about your emotional state, not appearances. So remember when you find yourself obsessing about something that someone said, just remember that you are impossible to offend, find a way to laugh it off, or if it is something that you can work on, get to work.

Also, one of the things you have to look for is people that you reflexively dislike which could be a manifestation of your inferiority complex. When you feel inferior to somebody it is an odd sensation of either wanting to supplicate to them or instantly hating them, sometimes oscillating between both states.

If you notice that whenever you see someone who's attractive and you start being critical of them in your mind, you will likely feel some degree of inferiority. One time I had a guy at my gym walk across the whole gym just to tell me "I find you ugly." Now I'm going to go ahead and brag (please roll your eyes while reading this next line), I have the body of a Greek god and I regularly get asked if I model.

Brendon: Greek god or not, Bill is in decent shape.

William: So when he did this I interpreted his actions as "Wow, he found me so attractive and that made him feel so insecure, that he walked across the whole gym in an attempt to make me feel insecure."

Arrogance aside, there was something about the way I looked that day which triggered a deep feeling of inferiority in him for him to walk across the gym and say something in an attempt to ruin my day.

This is also an example of how a strong frame interacts with getting attacked. I didn't let his inferiority complex make me feel insecure. Rather I just took his actions as further confirmation that I am attractive. Remember the people who have the strongest frames are the ones who aren't easily offended and interpret everything as a compliment.

I know I've repeated that line several times, but repetition is a foundational element in building a strong frame.

Jealousy

Brendon: The first thing to say about jealousy is that it's very important to understand what jealousy and the feelings of jealousy really are. There's a lot of confusion around this emotion in our culture. Many explanations of jealousy point to why it's negative, or will position jealousy next to envy and why one is potentially beneficial and the other is negative.

For the purposes of this book and this discussion, we're going to define jealousy basically as a feeling of frustration that arises when one witnesses something another person does and feels they cannot do it themselves.

There is a potentially positive way to handle that feeling, and there is a very, very negative way to do it. And the first way that we're going to explore jealousy is by talking about its potentially positive qualities to make sure that you understand how this is different from its negative aspects.

So Bill is a common guest on a program on SiriusXM Satellite Radio. He's gotten some notoriety from it. He gets attention from it. He's a great guest. They invite him back often. I'm jealous of that. I'm jealous because I would like to be on that radio program, but my life situation, not living in a location that allows me to be on SiriusXM Radio, nor knowing the people who would invite me onto that program is what's preventing me from being able to be in that situation myself. That's what's making me jealous. However, that jealousy is only fueling my motivation to want to put myself into a situation that would allow me to do something like being on SiriusXM. So I'm taking those emotions and I'm making them positive because it's all about my situation and circumstances, not about who I am. In fact, since writing this segment, and the recording of this audiobook, I've made the move to New York. I put jealousy to work *for* me.

The negative aspect of jealousy is probably one many people reading this book experienced potentially in high school. Many people reading this experienced something like this in their formative years: in high school, they were attracted to a member of the opposite sex that only had eyes for the head cheerleader or the captain of the football team. That's the stereotype anyway. Perhaps the reader made a judgement that the head cheerleader or captain of the football team possessed qualities that they did not, and couldn't have. That is a very, very negative emotion and negative spot to be caught in. It destroys your frame. It destroys your inner frame and it removes you from being able to create meaningful change in your life and the world by enforcing your frame, not only on people outside of you but on yourself.

William: The most insidious part about jealousy is that jealousy masks itself as a series of other emotions which include rage, anxiety, fear, and apathy, which are all frontmen for jealousy.

Brendon: Or depression.

William: I got really jealous that this girl I dated in high school was out hanging out with one of my guy friends, and I came home in a blind rage and my dad pulled me aside. He said, "What's wrong?" And I told him what the situation was, and he said, "Oh, so you're jealous." And I quickly said, "No, no, I'm not jealous," and then proceeded to describe the situation to him.

Brendon: I'm not jealous. I'm just going to kill this guy!

William: That's exactly how it went. My dad, he sat me down, he said, "Son, you need to not shame the emotion because when you shame the emotion, it builds power and it evolves into hate."

Brendon: Once again, let's point this out, that responding to the frame is reinforcing your feelings of inferiority and inability to make meaningful change in your life. That shows you, just to return to the earlier principles of the book, that you are caught within that frame. Reacting to the frame catches you within the frame. People who react to frames fuel them and then are caught within them.

William: The implicit assumptions of the frame were that my ex-girlfriend would like my guy friend more than me because I felt inferior to him. But that level of emotional transparency was impossible for my hormonal high school self. That's the reason why many people have a problem with jealousy, because admitting that they're jealous comes with admitting they feel inferior which is a hard pill to swallow. So it's much easier to feel indignant, rage, and hatred than it is to say you believe that you feel unworthy.

So the key is to not shame the emotion by admitting that's what you feel, jealous. Next is to admire the characteristics in the person that makes you feel jealous rather than hate them for it. Admiration is a virtuous form of envy. Envy is us noticing the good in another that we know we are also capable of achieving.

You will notice that it is those who we are closest to that inspire us with most the envy. That's because we find ourselves in an unspoken competition with people who are similarly situated. I am jealous of other comedians, I'm not jealous of tech billionaires. I'm not even jealous of comedians like Dave Chappelle and Chris Rock, I'm jealous of people who are slightly ahead of me in the comedy circuit.

Rather than letting jealousy cripple me, I choose to admire my competition, ask them questions, and appreciate their journey and appreciate the ways we are different and the same. Well, I do that for all the people I don't hate and the people I do hate are grossly undeserving. Just playing! That was my jealousy talking.

One of the things that you will be drawn to do whenever you're jealous is to find and attack their differences from you rather than appreciate them. See, when you attack them, you are basically reinforcing the jealous frame, which is a frame built around your own inferiority. So anytime you're actively trying to minimize somebody else's greatness, you're reinforcing the frame that they are superior to you.

When we are jealous we try to write a narrative on the reason why they were successful, maybe it was something we didn't have access to, in order to diminish their success and take the responsibility off of us.

Brendon: We're trying to remove the locus of control from ourselves and abdicate responsibility for the circumstances of our own lives.

William: Exactly. To keep the conversation relevant to personal history, there was one time in Chicago that a few comedians I know got a show at the Laugh Factory comedy club that initially I felt that they did not deserve.

I said to myself, "Oh they got the show because they were women.

The Power Bible

Women have an easier time getting spots in comedy because there are so few of them." This was the general consensus in my group of friends, whether or not it is true, it was what we believed.

Later, I investigated my premise and realized that there were other factors that were far more substantial to them getting a show. It turned out that they hung out at the club all the time. They offered value to the club by painting rooms and helping with events. They nurtured relationships with people who could give them opportunities at the club.

My co-producers and I followed their blueprint, and after we figured out what they did, we ended up with our own show at The Laugh Factory. If we had just settled with the belief that they got their show at The Laugh Factory because they were women, we would have never situated ourselves in a way to get the same result.

Brendon: How people who feel these emotions react to them is very important. Understanding how emotions react to one another and how new emotions are produced, and what actions these new emotions cause, can help you "see the matrix."

So as an example, Bill said responding out of jealousy is reinforcing feelings of inferiority. That is true. And let's go back to Bill's story about the Nazi video. Instead of appreciating that black people are just different and there are individuals who are black that are superior and have qualities that allow them to succeed; some inferior feeling white people decide to attack the idea of successful black people. But, the feelings that produced the attack, like the video, are feelings of inferiority. And rather than allowing the person who created the video to feel better about themselves, it only reinforces their feelings of inferiority.

This is how a dark circle of inferiority and shame can get started, because responding to the frame only captures you further into the frame.

Falling into a cycle of being within a negative frame doesn't just happen with jealousy, but with each negative emotion.

William: The expression "Don't compare yourself to other people" is banal. It's impossible not to compare yourself, your brain has billions of mirror neurons that exists so we can learn from others by comparing ourselves. So rather than cutting off your leg to avoid an infection, learn how to treat the infection.

How you do that is to look into the person you are jealous of. Look for the underlying character traits that helped them achieve their goals. Come up with a strategy that utilizes the new information you've learned.

Brendon: In Jungian psychology that is known as your "shadow gold."

Anger

Brendon: The feeling of anger is important to understand because anger is a primary emotion. It's a motivational emotion. It's actually one of the oldest emotions that has ever evolved in any living being. Millions and millions and millions of years ago, reptiles were the first ones who felt anger. And many of them, unfortunately, can only experience the feeling of anger because the medulla oblongata, where anger occurs, is the only part of their brain that is active & developed.

Anger is probably the second emotion after the emotion of fear to evolve. Why did it evolve so early? The answer to that question is pretty simple. Anger is a very motivating emotion.

People ball their fists, people punch pillows. People who get very angry do very crazy things when they are trying to handle that emotion. It's an emotion that requires a release. In this way, like other "negative" emotions, anger can also have positive qualities. Anger has allowed people to take action that has improved their lives and the lives of everyone in their communities by doing things like, stopping a bad guy, or going and killing a mammoth so that everyone can eat.

Anger is a motivating emotion. The problem is that undirected anger can destroy things in your life, your frame, and the lives of others. Anger can prevent you from holding a positive frame internally which in turn prevents you from enforcing a positive frame externally, particularly when it becomes the feelings of frustration, which is anger coupled with the feeling of inferiority. So particularly the feeling of frustration, which is a feeling of anger, is destructive to your frame and to the world around you because it reinforces the feelings of inferiority.

William: Anger is a powerful motivator but it's not nuanced. So anger could be what prompts you to confront your boss to talk about how you need a raise but it might also get you fired during the discussion.

Frame control is about having a panoramic view in order to have an effective conversational strategy; anger narrows your view until it blinds you. Anger can be effective at coercing people, but it comes at a social cost as anger erodes the trust of those who witness it.

Brendon: Anger is an emotion that demands compliance from people to whom it's being shown. This is because others can easily recognize the feelings of anger within someone else.

It's uncomfortable to be around someone who has a lot of anger if you yourself are not angry about the same things. It'll cause you physical discomfort. If you can handle your anger, if you can accept your anger and focus it, it can make you very effective, and channeling it positively can reinforce a very strong frame.

A good way to think about it is by imagining a child who is about to stick a fork in a light socket and a parent yell at them. That yell doesn't come from a feeling of shaming the child. That comes from a feeling of fear and then anger to demand compliance from the child because the parent knows what'll happen if they don't stop the child. People display anger because they want compliance, even to their own self. And if that compliance is in the best interest of both parties, it actually is a very powerful use of emotion. But if it's only in the interest of one party, it could destroy social relationships and reinforce inferiority.

William: When compliance is not given, it magnifies the powerlessness of the angry person. The power of anger is in its implicit threat. That threat is "I will hurt you if you don't listen to me." If the threat is exposed as an empty threat, it will no longer be respected.

Brendon: This is exactly correct, and it's why one should not ignore their own anger. You don't have to take the most immediate action that anger would like you to take, but you should take some action even if that action is deciding to feel the emotion and wait patiently until it passes. Ignoring your anger will make you begin to reinforce to yourself that your anger is empty, and will therefore undermine your own frame.

Fear

Brendon: Krishnamurti wrote a book which was the culmination of a series of lectures he gave on fear simply known as On Fear. Fear is the first emotion that evolved and it evolved probably first in mollusks in the ancient Ordovician epoch. The feelings of fear evolved as a reaction in the ancient brain to incoming data that something was about to kill the creature. So fear is a deep, deep, deep emotion that runs the foundational "background programming" in your brain.

When you see videos of cats jumping with fright at a cucumber next to them, it's because their brain is wired to respond to a cucumber the same way that the cat responds to a snake, because snakes could kill you very quickly. So it's important for a cat to react.

Fear is an emotion that has served all creatures for millions of years, but the environment that we live in today does not respect the use of fear in the same way that it once did. It doesn't mean that fear is not important. What it means is that the signal that fear gives to you, the signal that you receive from the feeling of fear, once pointed toward avoiding situations that could actually end your life. But in the circumstances we live in today, that is not the same. The signal that fear gives doesn't correspond to the actual level of threat you're facing from a scary situation most of the time.

Going into an interview is actually a very odd thing to do when you look at it from an anthropological, evolutionary perspective. At no point in primordial human history did a lone individual need to leave the safety and security of their own people, go to a completely different location inside of a strange temple or building where only strangers existed and prostrate themselves before those people in order to try and gain acceptance into their tribe. Probably in ancient history that only happened when people had absolutely terrible life situations and the only other choice was death. And many times people died in the end because they either weren't accepted or they were accepted and killed anyway.

The reason I bring this up is because if you're going into an interview and have lots of feelings of fear, that is completely natural but it destroys your frame. That fear prevents you from acting boldly, acting with confidence, displaying confidence to those people because it reinforces feelings of inferiority and vulnerability, creating anxiety. It can invoke every negative emotion possible. You can then later, if you respond to that fear, feel angry at yourself, angry at your life situation, and only continue to reinforce feelings of inferiority. Fear is a useful emotion and a powerful emotion for you to try to learn to contend with.

In my life, I've experienced a lot of fear in a lot of different ways. I'll give two stories about fear.

The first is that through a whole bunch of life events, I ended up becoming homeless in Colorado for the better part of a year, back in 2014. And it was challenging and I felt lots and lots of fear for many different reasons. I would feel fear daily. I had a lot of friends in Colorado and I was able to stay with a lot of them. It was also summer time so I could sleep in the back of my pickup truck.

I was confronted every day by the feelings of fear: How was I going to pay my bills? Where was I going to sleep that night? What was I doing with my life? Where were these things going? Fear at the idea of being discovered by the police, sleeping in my car on the street. Fear of my friends discovering my circumstances and having to deal with the social fallout. I played my homelessness pretty close to the vest and didn't want anyone to know exactly what was going on with me. There was a lot of fear, and the only way that I learned to deal with it is by trying to find the smallest amount of space in my life that I knew I had control over. In the face of all this fear and uncertainty, I had to remind myself what in my life I *did* control, and what meaningful change I could affect within that locus of control. And that's very challenging, but it's very important. You have to stay sold on yourself.

The way to confront fear is not by running from it immediately, it's by analyzing it, accepting it, looking at it and trying to understand what it's trying to tell you and then responding to it as one would respond to any threat, saying, "I see this as happening. What is it trying to tell me? Do I accept what it's trying to tell me?" Do I accept the message?

Sometimes it's very appropriate to listen to fear. Let me tell you another quick story. Years ago, my family lived in the woods in the Manistee National Forest for almost an entire summer. We lived in a giant tent. I've had a very eclectic life.

William: Prepared you for being homeless.

Brendon: Haha that's true! Well, one night I was walking back from the Little Manistee River, which ran right through the property on which my family had the tent. It was dark and I was walking on forest trail, and it's hard to describe, but I suddenly felt like I was being watched. There was nothing that gave an indication that was happening. I didn't hear any noises, I didn't see anything move, I just suddenly felt—the words in my brain were "something is watching me." I suddenly became terrified, but there was nowhere to go on this trail at night.

I pulled out a Ka-Bar knife which I was carrying with me and slowed down while trying to listen or see if I could tell if or what was watching me. As I walked down the trail, I continued to feel like I was approaching something and I wasn't sure what it was. It was dark, but I could see pretty well and didn't see anything on the trail. Just as I slowed down and at the moment where it felt the most intense in terms of something watching me, a very large animal—and I don't know to this day what it was—suddenly leapt up from just off the path next to me and ran as hard as it could into the woods away from me. It was probably a deer, but I heard it snapping branches and running and huffing. The animal was probably easily more than 200 pounds. I could tell it was heavy. I was overcome with a primordial fear and ran as hard as I could away from the animal. I don't know what it was, but I ran hard all the way down the trail, probably a half a mile back to my family's shanty.

That was a moment in which fear served me. It served me and it served the animal, it served both of us, because that animal was large, and if I had gotten in a fight with it I could have easily been killed. But let's not forget I was 160 pounds myself and I used to wrestle in high school. I had a knife on me that was built to kill things. I was as dangerous to that animal as it could have been to me. Fear served both of us. So you need to have a dialogue with fear to understand what it is trying to tell you. In that circumstance, it told both of us "We don't know what the other one is, it's probably good if we just both go," and that's exactly what happened.

But there are times when fear is making a mistake in telling you that you could risk losing your life, just like in the interview. Could you risk your life conceivably going into a strange building to talk with strangers about getting a job?

Conceivably you could. It's a very strange circumstance when you break it down to its most elementary parts, but it doesn't serve you any longer. And if you respond that way to many different circumstances in your life the way that you would in the primordial past, you'll be stuck inside a box of fear and that will only reinforce your feelings of inferiority and inculcate a very weak frame.

Examine your feelings as another data point, not as the entire set of data. Use reason and have an internal dialogue to investigate your feelings and see if they should be obeyed or if you should decide to act a different way. Retain your control and you'll retain your frame.

William: Brendon's story reminded me of when my best friend Joey and I got stranded in the mountains of Wyoming. All you have to know is that we had no cell phone service. There was no way for us to get his jeep out of the five feet of snow. We had cheap camping equipment that immediately broke. No one knew where we were because we said that we were going to camp in Montana but decided to camp in Wyoming instead. I was terrified. The scary thing about the situation was how quickly my mind began justifying doing things that I would have normally found to be morally reprehensible.

I have a joke from my comedy act that describes my thought process and what happened "My friend Joey, ended up having a seizure from hypothermia in the back of the cop car, and as I was watching him convulse in the back seat of the car, I couldn't help but think, if that had happened a few hours earlier while we were trapped out in the snow, I definitely would have eaten him"

Although that was a joke, it was a real thought. The fear had pushed me to a point of opportunistic paranoia.

Paranoia is hyper-destructive because it's an emotional state that can spread like a disease. Many of the worst things in human history were done when communities gave in to collective paranoia.

Paranoia can be benign, but if you continue to feed the paranoia frame, the more power it gets. Every action you make that validates your paranoia emboldens it. That's why you have to be vigilant when you are living in a state of fear because bad ideas will begin to make more sense. People who assume they will be moral during times of paranoia are the first to descend into vice. You must know that under certain circumstances you can feel compelled to do evil. Morality is tied to abundance and deprivation, at both extremes is where the justification for evil is likely to occur.

Take time to construct a character that can withstand uncertainty. That comes from experience and reflection. Many people have an intellectual relationship with fear, but the reality of fear is far different. Prepare for yourself to feel compelled to do evil. Prepare to tell your terrified self, no.

The Power Bible

In Love

William: Being "in love" is generally viewed as a positive emotional state. From a frame perspective, however, it's a negative emotional state. Being in love is associated with feeling powerless. "Falling in love" paints a picture of losing control.

Brendon: Love is a double-edged sword and we will discuss the positive aspects of love in a moment but understand that when you're in love, your brain is being flooded with chemicals that are meant to overwhelm your state and break your frame. The reason that this happens, and is meant to happen, is because you have literally millions of years of evolutionary programming and hundreds of thousands of years of human programming that are working in concert to try to get you to make a child with someone and be around them to protect that child and protect that relationship.

This is part of the reason why human beings have existed and flourished on the planet for so long, but those very same chemicals and triggers are meant to destroy your frame.

History is littered with examples of powerful people, both men and women, who have been overwhelmed by the feeling of being in love with someone else, and that emotional state destroying their life. Entire kingdoms have fallen apart and civilizations have collapsed because leaders have been in love with someone else and that love has caused them to shatter their frames and give up the behaviors and structures they need for success.

The classic story in the west is of Helen of Troy. Originally, Helen of Sparta. Paris, son of Priam, king of Troy, fell in love with Helen on a diplomatic trip to Sparta. Helen was the wife of the king of Sparta, Menelaus. Paris fell in love, as did Helen, and rather than listen to reason, both followed their passionate love. Helen secretly left Sparta with Paris and went to Troy. What followed is a story told and retold in the western canon for thousands of years; Menelaus and Agamemnon launched "a thousand ships" and invaded Troy. The Trojan War left thousands dead, including Helen, Paris, and all of their loved ones,

Hector, Priam and even the greatest warrior of the ancient world, Achilles.

There might be no better example of the negative effects of being in love. If Helen and Paris had held their frames, rather than give them up to love, the whole disaster might've been averted.

William: Being in love functions as an addiction to a person. Much like a drug addict supplicating to the demands of their dealer, the person in love does whatever they can to appease the object of their desire. The difference between love and being in love is that being in love is built around obtaining and sustaining reciprocation. This is an anxiety-inducing goal as other people's feelings are impossible to control, and their true feelings will always remain somewhat hidden.

When you're in love there are pleasurable feelings that you feel when your feelings are reciprocated, it is easy to descend into madness when you fear that might not be. The strange thing is that the media and society glorify this descent. The relationship is seen as not being legitimate if you do not have "butterflies in your stomach" when in a room together, or separation anxiety when the two of you are apart. These tropes create an unrealistic expectation for the relationship, as any sign of comfort is a sign that you are less in love.

As we mentioned above, feelings like anxiety and jealousy are not good for having a strong frame. Being in love can make these emotions a common occurrence in your life. We talked about outcome independence in the inner frame portion. Outcome independence becomes increasingly more difficult the more in love you are with a person because you need them to stay or be in a relationship with you.

As we will discuss later on in the book, the person who has the strongest frame is the one who cares the least. So the most in love party will be the one who has the weaker frame and advocate for their interest with less intensity. The first one to back down from a fight is that person who begins to experience their life through their lover's demands, living not for themselves but with the goal of sustaining the relationship.

The Power Bible

What you must realize is that being in love is a type of trance. You have communicated to yourself over and over again that the person you are in love with is important to you. You might have even gone as far as to tell yourself that the feeling you are experiencing is evidence of destiny. You recite the story as if it were a myth, telling friends and family about your relationship.

You look for evidence in common interests and romantic weekends as proof that your love will indeed be forever. As you look at pictures of them you remind yourself that you love them and that they love you. All negative emotions and fights are just evidence of how much you care. For months, even years, you tell yourself and everyone around you that this person and your relationship with them is the most important thing in your life.

Brendon: Our culture tells us that being in love and having someone who loves you is the ultimate expression of success in one's life. However, this is simply not the case.

It's wonderful if you are feeling overwhelmed, in a positive way, at your feelings for another, but it is vitally important as someone who is attempting to gain success to build a strong frame. You should know that when you're in love, your frame is being attacked by your own body, by your own neurochemicals, and by your own mind. Have a strong focus and understand that your feelings are not real, they're being influenced by chemicals that occur in your brain, and those chemicals are impelling you to try and create a specific outcome. Doing this will be necessary for you to remain objective and hold a strong frame.

William: When I wrote this section I had just gotten out of a relationship where I was in love. We had made loose plans to live together, talked about getting married, and joked about the hardships that our kids might have. She took up my every waking thought. I experienced morbid anxiety about what I would do if anything bad were to happen to her. I experienced fits of rage and jealousy if I heard about her spending time with another guy. I spent more time worrying about the relationship than reminiscing about the good times we had together.

The Power Bible

No matter how much evidence I had that she loved me, it wasn't enough. I began to exist behind a filter. Weighing out if what I was about to say would make her happy or upset. This was strange for me as I am known as someone who speaks his mind. I would also find it difficult to tell her things she did that made me upset or I would tone down how upset her actions made me.

Put bluntly, my runaway feelings for her made me dishonest. I was not telling lies but I also wasn't telling the truth. All my words were measured so I wouldn't offend her. I rationalized this as "I'm lucky to be with her" but the problem with believing I was lucky was that it implied that I was not good enough and that's why I was "lucky." This process made me lose respect for myself. I spoke with less conviction. I felt less creative. I had defanged and declawed myself. I experienced my life as a character in her movie.

Knowing the right thing to do does not make you immune to failure. There were many other relationships in my life around this time where I was able to act with decisive authority, but in relation to her, I had a weak frame.

I want to make it clear that my emotional experience was my fault. All my anxiety, jealousy, anger, dishonesty was a result of me not living up to my own standards in the relationship. Your emotions are no one else's responsibility but your own.

Brendon: This is so real. I would encourage the reader to think about their own experience to understand the difference between love and being in love, and what it means when people say things like, "love makes you do crazy things."

I once waited outside of a music venue for a girl I was attracted to in the cold for two hours. Basically just waiting for her while she was probably going down on some dude in the band that just played in Ann Arbor, Michigan. Simply, those feelings destroyed my frame. So, I had to walk away from that situation with feelings of being a loser, with feelings of attacking myself, shaming myself for having gone through that situation. Whereas, someone who's not in love would probably just have said,

The Power Bible

"Well, I came here with this girl, she's probably blowing this dude, I'm just going to leave and I don't want to talk to that girl anymore." That's holding a strong boundary.

William: It's easy to be humorless when you're in love.

Brendon: Haha! That's true!

William: I want to further say that being in love, as Brendon said, is not a prerequisite for having a good relationship. There are many people who end up destroying an otherwise healthy relationship because they chase a feeling that cannot be sustained for a long period of time. They do this because culturally, we have made novel and obsessive love the ideal, and if the relationship ceases to deliver these feelings then it's no longer valuable. Evidence of comfort can also be perceived as evidence of falling out of love, grounds for terminating an otherwise healthy and sustainable relationship.

Brendon: Another negative aspect to being in love is that once you have that feeling; that strong feeling anchored in your mind, you can build a narrative around it that sticks with you for much longer. That's actually the more dangerous situation because there are people who are reading this book right now, who experienced being in love and were in love at one point in time with the person who they're perhaps still currently with - those feelings may no longer exist but because they existed at one time, and because we have so many cultural explanations around what love is, they're still serving this narrative with their life by staying with the person they no longer love simply because they had the feeling of being in love one time.

In that case, who really has frame in this situation is actually you who built the narrative in your mind years, maybe even decades ago; and you're not aware of it, you're still in your mind serving that narrative rather than serving your own frame.

William: The more you make decisions in the direction of a particular frame, the stronger the frame gets.

Postive Emotions

The Power Bible

Positive Emotional States

Brendon: Before we talk about positive emotions individually, the first thing that we should mention is that the foundation for all positive emotions is the feeling of self-confidence. And the feeling of self-confidence comes from a feeling of security. And security can be loosely defined as basically meaning that you just feel good. You feel decently good. You have no need to feel afraid, you're not worried about anything, and you're comfortable in the setting and situation that you're in.

So, for many people, that means familiarity with people, or the settings & situations they find themselves in. But self-confidence comes from the feeling of security, and in turn, that feeling of security comes from having an expectation of outcomes.

So just to give an example, if you're hanging out watching TV in your living room by yourself, which is something that maybe some of you do too often, you might have a lot of self-confidence and security in this situation. And part of the reason you might do it a lot is because you feel positive emotions around it. You don't feel threatened by others, you don't have to give answers to others, you know that you're going to be able to watch programs on Netflix or play video games and you're going to have control over that situation. And you know that at the end of that you're going to be able to go to bed and nothing bad will happen that you'll have to deal with that could lead to a negative outcome.

Now you might be tired of doing those things, but the foundation of that situation is one of security and self-confidence. And actually, it's probably serving you because you're able to continue to operate within it.

Now, for Bill and I, we've moved our circle outside of our comfort zone far enough where we are secure in settings that many people would be very insecure in. Bill and I could get on stage in front of hundreds or thousands of people and tell jokes and get them to laugh and basically lead the attention of all of these people. You know, public speaking is the number one fear in the world that people have. We have the competence to do it because we've gone through it a lot. We failed a lot, but now we have security and comfort because we know what we can do and which of our actions will lead to what outcomes. So the foundation of all of these emotions, these positive emotions that we're going to talk about come from having a sense of security and self-confidence, and having these positive emotions are only possible through having a sense of self-confidence and control and security.

William: The more confident you are the easier it is for good emotions to arise.

Brendon: I think that's fair to say.

William: A person who is confident not only has more access to joy but the joy they experience lasts longer. It's because they have created a strong inner frame that can protect good emotions. We are rarely emotionally blank. We tend to experience feelings at all times that we perceive as positive or negative. Even in the dull monotony of life, we either experience low-grade anxiety or low-grade contentment.

Self-confidence is a police force that both protects and amplifies good emotions, while also getting rid of negative ones.

Brendon: Partially, this is because the ability to create positive emotions comes from someone's sense of control. If the only time you feel joy or expect to feel joy, for example, which is an emotion we'll talk about in a moment, is when good things happen to you, you're actually removing your ability to create joy in your own life and placing it outside of yourself, for the world to create joy for you.

Joy

Brendon: The first positive emotion we'll talk about is the emotion of joy. Joy is an appreciation, it's excitement, it's a feeling of expansiveness and of pleasure that comes from existing. The feeling of joy can be novel joy, fun, good feelings in the body. All of those things are the feelings of joy. Because of these reasons, joy is the most contagious feeling for enforcing strong frame.

If you are having a joyful frame at life, at the moment, in whatever you're doing, it is intoxicating for people to filter into. No one is going to turn you down because doing so is going to cause them to feel very negative emotions and they're going to want to filter *into* the good time that you're having.

William: An easy way to experience an abundance of joy is to lower your bar on what amuses you. The higher your bar of amusement the more difficult it will be for you to make yourself happy.

This is why children are so happy because all they need is an empty box to have fun.

Brendon: Think about children and babies. Babies can find joy by just looking at their own hands for a long period of time. We all still have access to joy like that.

William: Also gratitude for the mundane helps you stay in a constant state of joy. I smile in the morning and appreciate the fact that I can pee without issue. Your being able to pee is a rare event in the universe.

Everything you take for granted has an expiration date, and once that time comes you will never be able to experience those things again.

Brendon: A good way to get in the habit of appreciating the things that Bill just mentioned is getting into a daily gratitude practice. If you sit down with a notebook or simply with yourself and count off small blessings in your life and things that you feel gratitude for just 5 to 10 minutes a day, studies show this profoundly increases the amount of joy that you'll have in your life.

William: An easy hack for your anxiety is to be thankful for your worries. All your worries are built upon blessings. I had my computer die in law school a week before finals; I couldn't help but feel thankful for my worries. The problem of losing my notes was built on so many blessings. I was in law school, I had a laptop, I knew how to type, I knew how to read, life was good.

Courage

William: Courage requires fear. You must be afraid of something to experience the virtue of courage. When you take steps towards what you are afraid of, you are granted the gift of courage. Which provides you with euphoric feelings that gives you a strong frame. Acting courageously is bold and being bold is an integral part of having a strong frame.

Brendon: This is a powerful emotion for exactly those reasons. Courage is a physical emotion. And the courage that you feel is actually contagious to other people.

If we study history, we learn about people who were in terrifying situations and yet decided to act in a way that from an outside perspective would be against their own interests but for something they believed in, those people ended up being leaders. Think of the people like Martin Luther King Jr. and Rosa Parks, even the movie *Braveheart,* you can see examples.

We write stories and movies and biographies of people who do these kinds of things because the energy that it takes to act in the face of that kind of fear in those circumstances is worth telling stories about. And you have the ability to do this in your own life.

Enthusiasm

Brendon: Enthusiasm is excitement for something external that is outside of yourself. It could be excitement at something you're doing as well, but it's a prosocial emotion. Enthusiasm can be a display of positive energy put into something that someone else is doing.

Enthusiasm is actually a really powerful emotion because it *does* get people to want to filter into your frame. There's a comedian that Bill and

The Power Bible

I know in Chicago who is a very good-looking guy, and in the world of comedy being good-looking works against you. And he could easily have a lot of people hate him, but he's so enthusiastic for everything that anyone else is doing. He's always congratulating people and messaging them and saying, "Hey, it looks like that went really well. Really excited for you. Happy to see that you got this opportunity. It's really awesome. Looking forward to seeing what happens for you." He's so enthusiastic and encouraging that it's impossible to be angry at him.

Because of his enthusiasm, it's impossible to be angry at him and it's impossible to stay angry at him when he gets an opportunity that you know might have come his way only because he's good looking. Because he's so enthusiastic for everything that happens for everyone else, it feels like you need to reciprocate it for him. Enthusiasm is just a really good way for you to put positive energy into the world and maintain a frame control on a social situation that occurs outside of yourself.

William: Implicit in enthusiasm is the spirit of optimism. Optimistic people have strong frames because they believe life will unfold in their favor and since so much of life is a self-fulfilling prophecy, these people tend to be relentless in their pursuits, eventually getting what they want.

Enthusiasm functions as armor against rejection. This is an integral part of being properly persistent. Proper persistence is consistently offering value to a person, by way of good emotions, until they get into the emotional state of wanting to give you an opportunity. Persistence is done with a smile, and although pushy, is not done with trying to get someone to do something they do not want to do. Sometimes what feels like a bad idea for a person in one moment is a great idea in another, persistence takes advantage of the fact that people's minds are malleable.

Positive Fear

Brendon: This might be confusing because we defined fear as a negative emotion previously. Here's the thing, if you're reacting to fear, it's very negative. If you're feeling fear because something is scary and you're acting in response to it, not reactively, but proactively, that is actually a very positive emotion.

You know, climate scientists are every year, more and more seriously, and thoroughly banging their drums and pulling out megaphones to talk about the impending perils of climate change. This is a healthy fear. The negative fear is America's reaction by ignoring that dangerous message. We do so at our own peril.

The healthy fear is the fear that countries like Germany have taken by attempting to build more and more carbon neutral energy sources. That is a healthy fear. If you know that a hurricane is going to arrive in three days time, it's a healthy fear to have to motivate yourself to leave or to batten down the hatches and prepare to stay.

Now, this is different than acting out of courage, courage is taking action in the face of direct fear to defy that fear. If a bear runs out of the forest, courage might be confronting the bear. Positive fear is running away from the bear. There are situations that call for courage and there are situations that call for positive fear. And positive fear is actually a good emotion because it can save your life and it can filter people into your frame and help you enforce a frame that keeps you up.

William: Another element of positive fear is the transmutation of fear into strength. Fear is the most powerful emotion. Mothers have lifted cars off their children out of fear. Every Congressional Medal of Honor recipient performed heroic feats because they were afraid of what would happen if they didn't act. People misuse their fear by allowing it to paralyze them.

Fear is a form of passion. Every time I am faced with something I truly don't think I can do, I use my doubts to energize me. This has aided me in lifting over three times my body weight. I use my doubt that I cannot lift the weight as fuel to my make me stronger. The process I use to do this can most easily be explained by the Sith Mantra from Star Wars.

The Power Bible

"Peace is a lie. There is only Passion.
Through Passion, I gain Strength.
Through Strength, I gain Power.
Through Power, I gain Victory.
Through Victory, my chains are Broken"

Peace is a lie, you will always have doubts. You can channel those doubts into a passion. Sometimes this passion takes the form of anger. Anger with myself for not believing. Anger with myself for being afraid to fail. Anger with myself for being weak.

At this point, I start breathing deeply into my diaphragm. Allowing the waves of anger and energy to wash over me. At this point, I grab the bar and rip the weight off the ground.

This doesn't have to just be used for weight lifting. It can be used to get you off the couch. To get you to speak up in front of a crowd. To sustain yourself during a run. To have you not fold during a negotiation.

Faith

Brendon: The positive emotion of faith should be delineated from any sort of the negative feeling of hubris, which would be a belief in oneself without any kind of a foundation. Now, faith is simply that you don't know the outcome yet, you're not sure what the outcome is going to look like yet, but you're choosing to act *as if* the outcome that you're aiming for is going to happen due to your actions. That is the feeling of faith.

William: Faith in yourself and not circumstance, puts you in a position of strength. As James Allen wrote in *As a Man Thinketh* "Circumstances do not make a man, they reveal him." Faith is the act of believing in the person you are to find a way to succeed. It takes you out of the need for a particular outcome and makes you focus on your own self-reliance.

Putting you in a mindset that depends on your ability to be resourceful. At the core of this book is a concept of self-belief. Knowing that even if you do not know how to solve the problems in front of you, there will be a future version of yourself that will.

Love

William: The primary difference between being in love and love is that love's goal isn't reciprocation. Love's goal is the well being of the individual it's directed towards. Since love does not require reciprocation it allows you to be persistent in a way that would be difficult if you were afraid of losing reciprocation.

Think of a mother insisting her kids to do homework and to eat healthy. She doesn't care that her kids might be frustrated with her asking them to do this because her goal isn't their affection it's their well being.

Love is about doing what you believe is best for the people you love.

Brendon: I think the way that we want to define love here is being a strong feeling of appreciation that is transpersonal.

The concept behind a transpersonal feeling of appreciation is this: you are willing to go to lengths outside of your ego and have no self-investment in any kind of outcome. So, a good example is a mother who has suddenly gotten so much strength they lifted a car off of their child who's stuck underneath. That's something that would never happen with the exception of the fact that their body is telling them so strongly that they have to act to save someone they love very deeply.

Love is a strong transpersonal appreciation for another person and it can happen not just with parent and child, although that's a direct example, it can happen between any number of people as well. Bill and I are friends, I have a lot of love and appreciation for him, very little that we do as friends has any self-investment in any kind of outcome. Bill doesn't have to be any specific type of way for me to feel OK about myself. We joke around, we make fun of each other, we make jokes about ourselves or one another. If Bill called me and said he needed to talk to me at two in the morning, I would take the phone call.

The Power Bible

If he said I needed to fly out to wherever he was in order to help him with something that was really important, I would go and do it and I know that he would do the same for me and that's because we have a transpersonal appreciation for one another. Even though he might ask of me things that cause me stress or problems in my own life, I would go and do it. And that is why love can develop such a strong frame within you, because you are independent of the outcome and the feeling that you're working from can give you strong determinations.

That is the same reason we said earlier in the book why love can be negative. Love has been known to cause people to change their lives entirely, and even change the world. There are men and women who had never done anything meaningful or successful in their life, but when they found someone of the opposite sex who they were in love with, who challenged them to be their best self and do meaningful things in the world, they literally went and changed the world. These are the powerful results of someone having a transpersonal appreciation. When this happens the frame that is created from those feelings is unstoppable. This frame can even go past the point that any other frame would want to stop in order to preserve the self.

William: Being in love is often self-focused; the underlying questions you are trying to answer are "what does this mean about me?" or "what does this mean if this person who I find so attractive likes me?"

Love is not about your self-image. It's not about your identity. It's rooted in actions not feelings. Whereas being in love happens in the imagination, love is shown by a person's actions. A person who has a clear goal and wants nothing in return becomes infallible.

Frame Control in
Relationships

The Power Bible

III. Frame Control in Relationships

Intimate Relationships

Brendon: Frame control is important to relationships because the person who has control of the frame within which the relationship exists not only controls what the relationship *is* but is also the one who designs where the relationship is going.

Many arguments and disagreements in relationships are actually the results of misunderstanding the frame of the relationship. Not having frame can be what's actually keeping you from talking with your partner about real issues in your relationship. If you're caught within your partner's frame it might be difficult or even impossible for you to have an authentic conversation because you have been defined out of being able to do so.

William: The person with the stronger frame in the relationship controls the structure of the relationship. The terms of the relationship have to, on some level, be agreed upon by both parties. These agreements are rarely ever expressly stated, and more than likely what you have is a series of covert contracts that create a complex relationship when layered on top of one another. This creates a relationship filled with unspoken rules and consequences for violating those rules.

Brendon: A lot of people talk about "the friend zone." This is a situation in which someone wants a romantic relationship, but can't achieve it because that's not what the other partner wants. However, rather than accepting this and finding a different partner, the interested person continues to pursue the other under the guise that the relationship is only platonic.

This kind of relationship creates a "covert contract." Covert contracts were originally identified by Robert Glover in his book, *No More Mr Nice Guy*. The principle is very strong and it's important for you to understand. A covert contract is a contract that is entered into by one party, which silently states "I will do 'x' for you, to get 'y' in return," and implies the other party's acceptance even though they're not aware. Once this is done, no one acknowledges the contract. This is important because people who get caught in the friend zone end up in a covert contract of their own creation without even knowing it. This happens because all of their romantic intentions are in disguise, hidden, so the other party doesn't see them as romantic overtures. It's almost as if there's a contract that exists that says "I'm going to try to spend time with you, be nice to you, be around you in order to pursue a romantic relationship with you," that's never made explicit.

So the object of this affection might think, "Oh wow, this person is really nice to me. They're super cool. They're spending time with me. They're giving attention to me. That's really nice. We have a great friendship." All it would take for someone to change that relationship is say, "Look, I want to be romantic with you," to make the covert contract explicit.

A lot of times the reason this "friend zone" happens is because the person pursuing a romantic relationship doesn't feel deserving of the person they're interested in; they don't feel high status enough, or are otherwise unaccepting of their own feelings. Consequently they're afraid to try and change the frame of the relationship.

William: People who find themselves in that situation have a low tolerance for social pressure. They place other people's needs above their own. Even when they bring up issues that they are having in the relationship to a third party, they tend to argue against their own interests. This takes the form of rationalizing the other person's behavior as being their own fault. Often people who do this do not know how to advocate for themselves.

Brendon: The challenge is that covert contracts act secretly, and don't change the *actual* roles in the relationship. When people try to get out of the friend zone it normally goes wrong because once someone tries to play a different role, the relationship ends. People trust others as long as they're playing a role in their life well. But once someone tries to play a different role, the trust goes away.

The Power Bible

William: You have to establish the new role you want to play. This can put a lot of stress on a relationship and sometimes can cause the relationship to dissolve. The person you're in a relationship with wants you to continue to play a particular role in their life, more often than not it is the role they chose for you to play. Every time your actions come in conflict with the role they have assigned you is an opportunity for that person to lose trust.

Here is an exaggerated example to highlight the point: If you had a janitor who was good at cleaning your office, but then one morning you come into the office and they had "cleaned up" the memo you had been working on, by adding citations and correcting grammar errors, you would feel violated.

Even if they did a good job, them acting like your secretary could be grounds for you to fire them. You would lose trust in them not because they were an incompetent janitor but because their behavior shows that they don't understand what you expect from them.

Another example of this is when your role changes relative to someone in your personal life, such as when a friend that becomes an employee. Whereas before they were a friend you might have been lenient about showing up late, now in your office you might have a stern talk with them for the same behavior. This could put added strain on the relationship because most people have a difficult time compartmentalizing their relationships appropriately. So even if they intellectually understand they are playing a different role, the emotional experience they are having is more in line with the previous role they were playing.

A girlfriend or boyfriend becoming a wife or husband can cause conflict because the expectations we have for a spouse are different than the expectations we have for someone we're dating. Arguments become more frequent when we do not communicate our change in expectations. It could be the case that some people don't know that their partner's expectations have changed *until* they have an argument.

The characteristics that make a person a good girlfriend or boyfriend are different from those that make a person a good spouse. For someone we're dating we might not care about how much they earn and we might like that they live a wild and adventurous lifestyle, but for a person we marry, we might want them to make a certain amount of money and enjoy reading rather than raving.

From this line of reasoning you can infer that someone can be excellent at fulfilling a certain role in your life, but that doesn't mean you should necessarily upgrade the relationship. A person might be an amazing friend but that might not mean they will be a good business partner. A woman might be an amazing girlfriend but that doesn't mean she will be a good wife.

A good exercise is to outline the important people in your life and determine the role they are playing, and what role you would like them to play and how you will go about making that happen.

Now when someone is trying to upgrade their relationship with you or exercise a new dimension of themselves that they previously had not shown in the relationship, you might feel angry or anxious. Although you might be justified in feeling this way. Take a step back and examine the costs and potential benefits. Look at how the changing relationship could actually be a benefit to you.

When someone is attempting to upgrade their relationship with you, look at the character traits they have that would make them good or bad in the upgraded role. How do they react under stress? Are they self-aware? Do they integrate feedback? How do they express anger? Are they someone who spending time with would benefit you? Are they honest? Do they have a frame that if you were to adopt would make you a better person? Do they have characteristics that would make them good at the upgraded position? Have they shown evidence of these types of behavior in the past?

If a person is of strong character and has a dynamic inner frame then it is worth entertaining the idea of upgrading the relationship or expanding their role. Initially, you will feel uncomfortable with the new relationship if you do choose to give them an upgraded role in your life.

This is your brain getting used to them playing a different role. Much of their behavior will feel forced and you might find that you have less patience for them than you would someone who just walked into that role.

Know that this is to be expected and allow the new relationship time to cement itself in a different category in your mind. This awareness will make you more patient as you get used to their new "responsibilities." Take time to explain that your expectations for the relationship will be different and therefore both of you will likely be more irritated with each other at the beginning. Making this known at the beginning will allow you both to have a grace period with each other.

Arguments

Brendon: Much of the time that people—not just in romantic relationships but in just about any relationship—are fighting, the real conflict is actually unstated because the fight revolves around the symptom rather than the real inciting incident or reason. Much of the time, people have different tactics to avoid addressing the real reason they're arguing because doing so would make them vulnerable. Sometimes both parties don't even know what the real reason at the center of the conflict is; remember that in covert contracts, both parties act as if it does not exist. So, it's sometimes impossible to actually bring up the real issue that's causing the conflict.

Even acknowledging it, once the underlying issue is brought up, could make someone very vulnerable and defensive. In an example from my workplace, I had a subordinate bring something up with my superior in an attempt to get me fired. That person was trying to reassert their dominance, and they could have been doing it to show *themselves* that they still have power in the situation, not just that they were trying to show me, or trying to get me out of the way. Showing themselves they still have power could be the real reason that this person behaved that way. However, if I had brought it up or if I pointed it out, it would've made them feel far more vulnerable.

William: Do not bring up the real issues of why you are fighting during a fight. This sounds counterintuitive but a fight is a frame battle gone wrong. The goal of a fight isn't to solve the problem but to dominate the other individual and gain compliance. When a person is in a belligerent state they are incapable of listening to any position but their own. If you try to solve the problem during this explosive state you might frame your grievance in a way that's not palatable or you might have your legitimate concern be treated disrespectfully.

There are also tactics people use to keep the fight from moving to a place where a resolution could happen. There are four forms this takes: violence, crying, silence, and removal.

Violence is not always physical but it is an aggressive stance or volume that implies the threat of physical violence. This includes screaming, throwing things, knockings furniture over, punching walls, cursing, and interrupting. When someone has this as their argument default, they are attempting to silence you with force. People who use this tactic are usually not self-aware and are afraid of the person bringing up an insecurity that they are running away from. This style of argument annihilates respect as it demands compliance through fear of violence.

What we recommend is that when a person is at the beginning of their belligerent fit, leave. This will make them angry but you are actually saving them from doing something that can't be forgiven. Many times when a person is in a violent state, they will say things that can never be unheard or do something that can never be forgotten, and in some cases forgiven. Give them time to exhaust themselves. Shut off your phone and wait a few hours before sending a written form of correspondence expressing your feelings about the subject and why you left. This will allow them to know what you are upset about and what you want to change without being interrupted or having your argument mischaracterized.

Crying is a powerful tactic in an argument. People do cry from being overwhelmed but criers use it to stop themselves from being held responsible for their actions. Criers will use their tears to stop a fight when they are being asked hard questions or being asked to do something that would be an inconvenience. This pattern of behavior is childish and likely a conditioned response to avoid taking responsibility.

What you do when a crier begins crying is to stop talking and wait until they are finished. Anything you say will only further encourage the emotional state. Be ready to hear things like "You don't care" "Why are you doing this to me?!"

Resist the urge to console them or to respond to what they are saying. Wait patiently until they have exhausted themselves. Once they stop crying, there will be one of three things will happen: either they will be willing to carry on with the dialogue and you can begin an honest communication or they will resort to the last two tactics.

Once again I am saying that a crier is someone who typically uses tears to avoid taking responsibility for their actions, and uses this tactic to gain compliance. A crier tends to cry when their argument has holes in it, or they have been confronted with facts that are difficult for them to argue against. In order for someone to be considered a crier they tend to cry frequently when arguing. Remember that crying in and of itself isn't necessarily manipulative, and it can be an honest response to a heated discussion, but if tears tend to fall any time they are in the wrong, and never when they are in the right, that *is* evidence of them being a manipulative crier. Many manipulative criers are not aware that they are crying to gain leverage in the fight, so labeling them a manipulative crier during an argument is not an effective tactic. Simply just sit there in silence and wait for them to tire themselves out before reasserting your position.

Silence or removal, both of these are tactics used to take back control of the frame by disengaging. Both are used when the person you're in an argument with has no intent of listening to your position. If they do re-engage you, they are doing so because they're expecting your terms to change due to the validation vacuum they created. Do not allow them to do that.

If a person regularly employs the silent treatment, for days or weeks, make it clear to them that you will stop the relationship if this kind of behavior continues.

The second method takes patience and you must look at what they are doing as a game. Understand that ignoring someone who's talking to you as if nothing is wrong is exhausting for the silent party. This is because you are not validating their silence frame and so they will begin to doubt if it's working. Do not address your frustration with them ignoring you because it will embolden them.

The silent treatment is also the easiest behavior to change out of the three. Belligerence and habitual crying are reflexive strategies that were probably learned during adolescence or earlier. The decision to cry or get loud and throw things, happen almost automatically, making the behavior difficult to change. The silent treatment is a more conscious decision and is easier for a person who habitually uses it as an argument tactic to stop as it only requires that they have a discussion with you. So do not be afraid of telling the person you are willing to leave if this behavior becomes a habit in the relationship, as the power to change is firmly within their grasp.

Brendon: This is important to take notice of, because this is how to identify manipulative argument tactics, something very difficult for anyone to do in the moment.

William: As with the entire book we want you to reflect to see if you have any of these types of arguing styles as your default in certain relationships. The easiest thing to do once a fight begins is to repeatedly state your position. Do not change your tone. Do not change your rhythm. Do not respond to them mocking you for repeating the same thing over and over again.

Don't allow the person to make the argument about something else. People will often, when they are losing a fight, try to make the fight about something else. Just say "That might be true, but what we are talking about right now is (blank)."

When you get past their avoidance tactics is when you can have a real discussion. Subconsciously, the person you are arguing with realizes this, and that's why they are trying to control the conversation and be avoidant by using these tactics. They are not necessarily Machiavellian, they just have developed coping mechanisms to get what they want in the short term.

Brendon: If you want an example of manipulative tactics, go watch the Jordan Peterson interview with Kathy Newman. The Peterson-Newman interview is a great example because Kathy Newman tries many different manipulative argument tactics on Jordan Peterson, who counters them expertly and maintains consistency of message & demeanor. He undoubtedly won that argument. Let's talk about the validation vacuums here.

William: A validation vacuum is where a person who regularly validates you stops. When somebody stops validating you, you will end up experiencing a myriad of emotions ranging from anger to sadness. These are all emotional states that contribute to diminishing your frame. So when you are in these states, when someone has pulled their validation from you, and you're wondering if they will ever interact with you again, you will end up questioning your own frame and even making arguments against yourself. Often, you'll put yourself in a less advantageous position when you two reconvene.

Many of the narratives that come out of a validation vacuum only exist because you need to justify why you feel the negative emotions you are experiencing. This is why you can talk to somebody who is in the midst of an argument with a lover, or close friend, and they make up a narrative of how the other person has always been abusive to them, or how that they never actually liked that person. The person is just responding to the vacuum that they're experiencing and so they need to come up with a narrative that fits the level of offense that they feel.

It's also important to remember that just because a person made you feel a certain way doesn't mean they intended to make you feel that way. The conflation of these two things can lead to someone mistakenly making their partner out to be a villain. In romantic relationships, we are hypersensitive to the actions of our partner. Something that they did out of ignorance might feel like it was done out of malice because we conflate how their actions made us feel with their intention.

Brendon: This is why you do not want to act out from the feelings caused by a validation vacuum; because anything you will do is caught in a reactive state and will only cause more distress. In fact, the tactic I use for myself when I'm in a validation vacuum is simply to tell myself, "Yup, I'm done. I'm no longer going to have anything to do with this person in my life. I'm just writing them off entirely. I'll never see them again. I'll probably never talk to them again," and just accept that.

Now, whether or not that happens is not up to me, it's up to them because I'm walking away until they want to come back and get back into my frame. This is why you'll see high-level business relationships, high-level romantic relationships, people who are used to playing the game and have strong frames, will sometimes fight back-and-forth and spend long periods of time not speaking with each other because they're jockeying for position by utilizing validation vacuums.

William: Two things to keep in mind. Do not re-engage someone until you have cycled through the emotions that are negative for frame, anger, jealousy, and fear are all horrible negotiating bases and might cause you to act in ways that aren't in your best interest.

Second, don't expect them to have the particular emotional state you would want them to have when you reconvene. Meaning if you feel they have wronged you, don't expect them to feel guilty next time you talk. Many people end up getting themselves upset again because they don't feel that the person is "sorry enough" or feels bad enough about what they have done. Someone who feels this way ends up getting stuck on the other's lack of an appropriate feeling, and the argument begins all over again.

Decide in advance whether the issue being discussed is a "deal breaker." If you have made the decision that the issue is a deal breaker for you, then you will have a stronger frame than if you find out it's a deal breaker during the argument. Do not do a false deal breaker, where you say the issue is a deal breaker for you, but when your partner doesn't budge you fold instead; that makes the other person lose respect for your word.

You need to keep cognizant of your anger and sadness cues. Are you beginning to raise your voice? Are tears starting to build? Are you interrupting them? Making personal attacks? Bringing the subject off topic?

When you notice yourself doing that, apologize for your behavior, take a five-minute break if you have to, and then return to the table. You want to stop a fighting frame before it has time to escalate.

Brendon: This is all true. I think it nails the subject.

William: Remember that most people's demands are malleable and are rarely static. So even if they say certain terms are non-negotiable at that particular moment, they might be negotiable later on. If governments can change laws, people can change positions. A change in context can make a formerly non-negotiable term negotiable. For example, how do you get a king to exchange his crown for a glass of water? Deprive him of water.

Sometimes a disagreement continues even after a person has been convinced of your position. This happens because the person who has been convinced does not want to lose face and would rather continue arguing than admit they were wrong. When you suspect that this is the case, say something like "I admire your intelligence and persistence on this point, but right now I don't know if we're really understanding one another, let's take some time to let our emotions die down."

By giving them a compliment before you disengage, they will accept one of your assertions. In general, once someone has accepted one of your statements as being true, it makes them more likely to accept your other assertions as also being true. Also, by disengaging, you put them in validation vacuum where they are more likely to be self-reflective about the argument. The statement about misunderstanding will be on their mind because it was the last thing you said. It's unlikely that they will come back and say "Yea, I was being purposely obtuse, you were right about everything." What will likely happen is that they will come back more pliant and willing to listen.

The Context of the Argument

William: Discomfort breeds conflict. If a friend or partner of yours gets mad at you for something that's minor, look at the context before marching into an argument. Are they hungry? Tired? Stressed? Hot? Cold? Sick? Think about the last time you got in a shouting match. Ask those same questions about yourself in that situation.

Our physiology influences our emotions. Often times we will come up with an emotional experience to justify our physiological state. A simple way to put yourself in an advantageous position is to make sure the person you're speaking with is well fed and rested before you talk about a serious issue.

It's worth remembering that homicides go up in every major city during the hottest days of summer. Our physiological state can motivate us to do the unthinkable, so take it into consideration when you're having a disagreement.

Think about timing as well. Are they picking fights with you at night after work? Give them time to unwind before you talk with them. You want to be aware of situations that cause them anxiety and what cues they give off about being anxious. You can sometimes tell if someone is anxious by looking into their eyes. If they feel anxious, study how you can bring them out of that mood quickly. Don't take it personally if they sound doubtful about your relationship at that moment. Remember many times it's the mood talking, not them.

Many people start off the day being anxious because they have had too much coffee and sugar. If this sounds like your partner or friend, try making them a breakfast that would diminish anxiety with less sugar, more protein, and less strong coffee.

Periodically ask yourself "how can I mitigate their negative emotional experiences." Same with yourself, always be thinking "What things can I do to mitigate this negative emotion?" Look to diet and exercise before existential answers. Don't tell a person to their face "I think you're hungry and that's why you're getting angry" it can sound patronizing and diminishing. Just understand that it might be the reason and have more patience with them at that moment.

Brendon: It's belittling to them. It's important that you simply notice it. It's important to notice how context affects conflict because not everything is always a frame battle. Sometimes people are just under stress and simply not good at managing their own emotions.

It's especially true for someone who's in a work context. When working in an office, it's especially good to remember why people are speaking with you, and why they're bringing up to you what they're bringing up to you and how they're bringing it up to you. Do they have a deadline? Are you unknowingly affecting their work?

The Point of View

Brendon: Accessing someone else's point of view is a game changer on an order of magnitude of increasing success with others, and getting others to accept your frame. Understanding where people are coming from and gaining a perspective with their point of view will change the way you negotiate. It'll change the way you behave in romantic relationships. It's going to help you succeed with others in ways that you haven't before and that's basically what Bill is identifying with understanding someone else's point of view. Are they hungry? What's their past like? How are they going to view events? How are they going to view what I'm saying to them now or what I'm about to say to them? How can I say it in a way that gets them aligned to my frame and so that they see it is a benefit to them?

William: When you feel like an argument is inevitable, begin reflecting on their point of view. First, look at their explicit incentives. For example, your son has been pestering you to buy them a car. He says that the reason he wants a car is to get to work after school. Look at the implicit incentive, for example, your son wanting a car to get out of the house and spend more alone time with his girlfriend.

James Altucher calls these The Good Reason and The Real Reason. By finding out what The Real Reason is you'll understand what they actually want and maybe find another way to offer a solution. Too many people just settle with The Good Reason and try to meet the other halfway, but it doesn't work because it's not getting at the heart of what they actually want.

You want to spend time imagining what it is like to be them. Go through the facts that they have shared about their life. Who they were in high school, whether they like their job. What are their fears, anxieties, hopes, dreams, values etc. Reflect on their mixed feelings about you, what they admire and what they dislike.

Reflect on who has authority over them in their life. What authors do they read? What do you think their therapists will say about the situation? What would their partner want? Finding out who are the authority figures over a person both living and dead is a powerful way of understanding why they do what they do.

You want to lose yourself in this process and become your opponent. If you do this properly it will bruise your ego. Do not assume that you both value the same thing. Many times people expect that others close to them value the same things and this is just not the case. Even similarly situated people have different values. Look at their actions for evidence of what they value.

If you get good at this you will become clairvoyant. You will be able to predict things others will say, how they will say them, how they will react to things you say. You will not be caught off guard by things they bring up. You will even feel an unspoken empathy for them because you understand them at their core.

After you finish this practice you want to then think about your own position. Meditate on why you want the things that you want. Go through all the questions that you came up with that they would throw at you. Come up with responses that would cater to some of them, but have you come out on top.

You want to do these in exactly that order so you have both empathy for their position but steeled yourself on your own. You will be able to answer their questions with poise and when you say you know where they are coming from it's not just lip service. At the end of the day, however, this book is about getting what you want, and your point of view is the one that matters.

Now, if you genuinely change your point of view during the reflection part of this exercise then don't be afraid of admitting that you changed your position and walking them through your train of thought. It will show them that you took the time to understand what it's like to be them.

"When we communicate with one another, and we feel that we've connected, and we think that we're understood, I think we have a feeling of almost spiritual communion. And that feeling might be transient, but I think it's what we live for." - Kim Krizan

Brendon: That's just so powerful. Understanding where someone is coming from and how, and preparing to move with them in conflict, discussion, argument, or any frame battle, this is the Tao of Jeet Kune Do of how to understand frame. Recognize that each person, each fight is its own unique set of circumstances.

To make a comparison, your skill as a martial artist displays your ability not how to throw the same kick, but how to throw that same kick given a completely different set of circumstances. And this is exactly what you need to be if you want to be a master of frame control and gain power over yourself or others. You have to duck and weave while enforcing frame given the changes in the environment and the players.

When working out another's point of view. Get out a piece of paper and write things down in front of you to make them explicit. It'll slow down your thinking and by looking at them and assessing the character of the person you're thinking about. This exercise will point out whether you're missing something that's potentially very valuable that you could use to understand their frame and therefore how to enforce the reframe.

A good exercise here is dividing a piece of paper into four quadrants. In each quadrant you write down "desires," then "fears," then "tools," and finally "unknowns." Write the name of the person you're outlining at the top. The idea is you then to outline a few things quickly: what does this person want? What are they afraid of? What resources or tools are they using to reach their conclusions? What's available to them? What's explicit to them? And finally, what's unknown to them?

If you can identify things that are unknown to them, it's a peek into their unconscious, they're 'blind to self'' Johari window. For example, if you know someone who thinks he's adventurous, but he's not adventurous, and you know that and he's not aware of it, that's the way you play "in the pocket." When boxing or MMA, the way that you fight is in "the pocket." That guy can't hit you because you're too close and he can't grapple, you're just in the pocket. You're throwing punches. He's got to back off. He's got to move. He's got to get around so he can actually connect with you. In a frame battle it's the same way. If I can play inside the pocket, no one is ever going to come in and try to attack and they're always going to be off balance. I'm challenging this guy constantly to be adventurous. He's never going to do it because he can't do it himself.

Difficult Times: Moments That Lead to a Lack of Frame

William: There are moments in life where it is difficult to hold frame. Times where negative emotions are abundant and it's difficult to see your role in the world. These times often coincide with a loss. Getting fired, being broken up with, getting ill and having someone close to you die are times where your frame might become fragile.

Brendon: Moments like this, what we call 'hard times' or 'difficult moments,' this is the time when reality is becoming the ultimate teacher again.

The Power Bible

Holding a frame is something that happens in your mind, and it happens in other people's minds. It's personal, it's also social, frame exists in many different locations but one place that frame does not exist is extra-personal reality. Outside of human perception, frame does not exist; reality is the way that it is. You might want to say that Kant called this 'noumenon' - it's the physical reality of the universe that we live and operate it in. It doesn't matter how much we believe that a meteor will never hit the earth and kill us, that will happen regardless of our thoughts, feelings, or opinions on it.

It doesn't matter how much we don't think an earthquake is going to destroy the city of Los Angeles, if the earth moves in such a way, it will happen. In this way, reality is the ultimate frame holder. It has the ability to shatter the things that you want to believe in.

You can believe that you are doing a great job at work and are being valued as an employee, but if there's a shift in the marketplace and management decides to dissolve your entire business unit then it doesn't matter what your thoughts or feelings were. It's important to understand this because there are two mistakes that you can make in this period of time.

The first is that you can think that your holding of the frame will change reality, which it won't. Or you can think that your frame was wrong, due to reality changing. Each of these things is a categorical error. You have a frame and reality has a situation and the two of them can vary independently. You could have had the correct frame about you and your job at work, you could have had the right model, you could have been doing valuable work but because the greater situation outside of yourself that you had no control over changed around you, it resulted in you losing your job. So, the mistake that you could make is believing that you needed to work in a different kind of way in order to ensure that you never got fired. That could lead to you doing bad work in the future and getting fired because of those reasons.

Frames and reality are independent of each other. This is why the most successful people use reality as a strong teacher, and incorporate disconfirming evidence from the world around them into their frames, making their frames stronger.

William: The fragility of your frame in times like these can be attributed to the fact that you construct narratives about what *should* happen. Whenever something happens that you did not anticipate or that you did not have control over, we feel as if our world has fallen apart. This is because our worldview, our inner-frame, has been shown to be fallible by having something we could not predict happen.

In these moments, where our world seems to be falling apart, is where a person with a dynamic frame thrives and those with rigid frames fall apart. Nassim Taleb talks about how human beings are Antifragile, a system that gains resilience and robustness from disorder. People who have a dynamic frame are antifragile while those who have rigid frames are fragile in times of hardship.

Brendon: Yes, I think that's a very good way of putting it.

William: There is also a loss of identity in these times. When you say "my girlfriend," or "my job," you are implicitly stating that these things are part of who you are and when you lose permission to call someone your girlfriend or boyfriend, or you lose permission to say you hold a certain position at your company, you feel as if you have lost *status*.

This is because status has to do with how desirable you are compared to other people. When you are in a relationship it is proof that you are in fact desirable, as it is assumed that the person you are dating desires you. The same goes with you having a job, your employer desires that you keep working there and that's why they pay you money. The more difficult it is to get and sustain a job where you work, the more status you derive from working there.

This is why job loss affects people in different ways. A person who received a lot of validation from society for where they work will suffer more of an identity loss than a person who doesn't get validated by society for where they work. A person who loses a job as a cashier at McDonald's isn't going to suffer from the same perception of loss in status as somebody who loses a Vice President position at JP Morgan.

The Power Bible

This is why there are stories of Wall Street executives killing themselves after losing their high-status position, even though from a financial perspective the job loss isn't as devastating to them as the McDonald's cashier losing their job.

Part of this is associated with the narrative that a person who works at JP Morgan creates about themselves. They put themselves in a trance where they believe that the reason why they are important is because they have a job at a prestigious company and have a prestigious position at the company.

It doesn't matter how balanced and self-aware the person might be, they will still be in a trance of self-importance about their position. When that narrative is stripped from them they will no longer feel like they are worthy of being important. This, combined with the fact that the people around them will treat them differently during their unemployment validates that narrative.

It is important to remember that status is relative. Yes, losing your job makes you lose certain privileges and status within a certain subculture but the vast majority of people don't care. With the exception of being a celebrity or being hyper wealthy, most people could care less about what you do.

Where jobs and relationship differ is that you have to go out and get another job as soon as possible for survival. With breakups it's different because many people believe right after a breakup that they will get back together with their former lover. That belief is not shared with many people who get fired or laid off; most people believe when they are fired that there is no chance of getting their job back. Second, is that you don't need to be in another relationship to survive.

The time between relationships can be perilous because you are existing in a validation vacuum. A validation vacuum causes anxiety, anger and self-reflection. Although these emotions are uncomfortable they ultimately lead you to develop a stronger frame if you can sit alone with your thoughts rather than run away from them by pursuing others immediately after the breakup.

The Power Bible

Brendon: Bill is describing a friend that everyone has: the serial dater. A person who goes from relationship to relationship but never really having anything solid. This person is attempting to capture a feeling that they have at the beginning of something, but every time they break up they never actually learn any lessons.

William: Our last bit of advice is to fight your instincts at times like these. You might feel as if you want to sit alone watching television for days. This is because you have experienced a loss and your brain is releasing cortisol and other anxiety inducing hormones. Remember, winning and losing are constructs in the mind but experiencing a win or loss does cause physiological reactions in the brain.

To combat the hormones that are being released in your brain during these periods you should engage in a lot of physical activity. Running produces a lot of endorphins and other hormones that make it easier to experience positive emotions. It's hard to feel desperate and hopeless when you're in the middle of a seven mile run or at the bottom of a squat.

Another thing to do is to label actions as "wins" rather than results. Make a goal of how many jobs you will apply for a day, once you hit that goal, reward yourself and pump your fist in the air saying

"Win!" The winner's effect is a real physiological phenomena and because the concept of winning is a construct in our mind, that we can produce on our own, by celebrating the small victories after a big loss.

The Power Bible

Macro-Cultural Frames

The Power Bible

IV - Macro-Cultural Frames

A: Status

William: Status is what bends the rules of the game. The highest status individuals have no rules enforced on them, while the lowest status individuals' lives are ruled by the whims of others. Billionaires have limitless opportunities, prisoners have zero autonomy.

Everything you hold dear can be taken from you if your status drops low enough. Your home, your children, even your right to shower alone, as with the case with prisoners. Many of us are unaware of the majority of our privileges because we tend to take so many of them for granted.

I want you to think about how people treat the homeless. Even when a homeless person tries to speak to strangers directly, they are not acknowledged. This highlights another nuance of status: A low-status individual can scream and have no one hear them, a high-status person whispers and it makes front page news.

It's not what is said, but who says what.

Not everyone's word is valued the same. In law school we are taught how to impeach a witness, which means attack the witnesses' credibility so that the jury doesn't weigh their testimony heavily.

The weight, meaning the cultural value of what someone has to say, is based on a myriad of factors. More people care what Kanye West has to say about climate change than climatologists; this is because Kanye's position as a cultural icon allows him to transcend the need to be an authority on the subject for his word to have a social impact. Meaning, people on a large scale discussing the legitimacy of his assertion.

Those who are the best at garnering attention, positive or negative, become the most culturally relevant, which gives their word more value in the cultural landscape. The more value your word has, the more people will feel compelled to act in accordance with it.

The Power Bible

A person's status can make an ordinarily sane person insane. For example, there are women who have broken into Justin Bieber's house in an attempt to have sex with him. Justin Bieber is not a bad looking guy but his looks are not what is compelling women to risk going to jail to have sex with him.

The more high status an individual is, the more they will change the behavior of those around them. People have burst into tears from being touched by a musician at a concert. Well reasoned individuals have lost their ability to speak in the presence of their favorite actor.

This is not because of the talent of the musician, nor is it because of the skill of the actor, it has to do with their status. You strip them both of their fame and have the musician play that same song at a local bar or the actor play the same role at a local theater, and no one would look twice. They might even believe they are doing the musician a favor by listening to their performance.

This works in the opposite direction as well. Many of the people who lynched blacks in the south were respectful and polite to the whites in their community. The people who are the greatest slaves to status are the unintelligent and weak willed. That being said, you should be vigilant with yourself, as none are immune to status's spell. When around high status individuals to make sure that you do not compromise your integrity when confronted with the primordial desire to conform to a high status person's wishes.

Your fluctuation in status will change people's behavior to you as well. Do not be upset or surprised by this when it happens, take advantage of it when it's working in your favor and laugh at it when it isn't. When you have no status you will be cursed with being invisible and when you have status you will be cursed with the inability to be invisible.

Brendon: This leads us to the concept of money, and its relationship to status, and macro-cultural frames. Money isn't quite the physical representation of power, because money is actually inefficient in many ways, but money is the attempt at storing value outside of goods and services. And it's a value that's exchanged for those things; it's the attempt to measure value through an external amount. It flows to people with status *because* the system values them.

William: And how would you describe wealth?

Brendon: Wealth is the accumulation of value over time.

William: The reason that wealth and money are intimately tied to the concept of status is that the person who is in possession of large sums of money can purchase privileges and access for themselves and the people around them.

People's awareness of your wealth or the potential wealth will make them more likely to listen to what you have to say.

Money is a form of universal status. Meaning that it conveys status that can be taken with you wherever you go in the world. For example, a nightclub owner has a lot of status in *his* club but when he goes to another city he doesn't have any status.

A person who is famous in South Korea but is unknown when he travels to America will therefore not receive any of the same benefits of fame. This is why money can be more powerful than fame, because for fame to give you access it requires that you are recognized, money gives you access because it's universally recognized.

B: Speech

William: The way you speak is one of the easiest ways to convey status. In America, a person with a refined British accent needs to do less than a person with a Mexican accent to be perceived as intelligent and wealthy. This is not fair, but this book is not concerned with what is fair, but how you can use unfairness to your advantage.

The reason why speech is such a clear indicator of status is because it's an honest signal. Unlike putting on a piece of clothing which you could happen upon in a circumstance that doesn't require you to come from a family with wealth, the way you speak can imply where you grew up and how much money your family had. The assumptions that are being made from how you speak can either paint a picture of prep schools and summers in the Hamptons or delinquency and gang violence.

Now we're not advocating that you start using a fake British accent, but be cognizant of the assumptions that you make when you're around someone who does have a British accent. Don't give them implicit authority just because they might sound more academic.

We also want to stress the importance of having good diction. A well-placed and uncommon word can be a powerful signal to the people around you that you're an educated and thoughtful person, it does not matter if that is actually the case.

The more positive people's assumptions are about your intelligence, the more susceptible they are to taking what you say as law. Practice also speaking clearly and enunciating words correctly. Get rid of filler words like "um," "ah" and "like" and replace them with pregnant pauses to give the illusion that you're crafting your sentences with care.

Be aware of when you get excited and anxious, both can lead to you changing your rate of speaking. Generally, the faster you speak the less likely people are to take what you're saying seriously. The people who we know to speak with a lot of casual authority speak slowly. Take for instance, Morgan Freeman or Neil Degrasse Tyson, both men take their time when they are speaking, and have even mastered the ability of speaking with passion while speaking in a slow and measured way.

C: Fashion

William: There is a trend where people say that you should not spend money on clothes and to instead focus on saving for a house. Now I wouldn't say that is bad advice but they are undervaluing the importance of having a dapper wardrobe. For most people will never see your home but everyone you meet will see what you are wearing.

Being in vogue communicates that you are socially aware, wealthy, and are desired sexually. All of these things are powerful implicit assumptions someone can draw from you without you ever having to open your mouth. Having a good fashion sense that fits your body type and the context will act as a social passport. Where you find other people would have to wait in line, you will be shown the back entrance.

Humans have communicated their power and role in society with the way that they were dressed since the dawn of man. Chieftains wore seashell necklaces, kings wore crown, doctors wear white coats, and judges wear gowns. What a person wears displays their role, status and even duties in society.

In order to know what is trendy, go to the places in your city where celebrities hang out. You don't have to go in, but just start looking at what people are wearing and more specifically how they are wearing the items they choose to wear.

For men, look specifically for men who have women around them, or look as if they usually do have women around them. This is because women's acceptance can be an honest signal that what the man is wearing is fashionable. Make sure you look at the way they are wearing their accessories and what accessories they are choosing to wear. Make sure when you're looking for a person to emulate that they have a similar body type to you.

The way the clothes fit is more important than the brand. From there go online and find clothing brands who sell similar styles to the ones you saw on your scouting trip.

This may sound like a lot of work, but the more work you do on the back end, the less money you will waste buying outfits that aren't cool. I also cannot overstate how much upgrading your wardrobe can make an impact on your life.

Understand that fashion is context specific. A cool outfit at a black-tie event will look ridiculous at the beach. You also have to take into account what you want to communicate about yourself in that situation. My current look is great for being a creative person that lives on his own terms but it would look wretched if I was a trial attorney. The look that helps me saunter past lines outside night clubs would keep me from ever getting in the front door of a law firm.

Ask yourself this question when leaving the house "What does this outfit say about me?" Get in touch with what each part of your outfit communicates. Think about the type of person you want to make an impression on when you are leaving the house. What are the types of qualities that they would be looking for in the role you're trying to fulfill? What articles of clothing or accessories are you wearing to paint that picture?

In the book Moral Tribes by Joshua Greene, he mentions a study where it was found that human beings distinguish each other based on clothing before race. They hypothesize that the reason this occurs is because prehistoric humans didn't encounter people of different races but they did encounter people wearing different clothes even within their own tribe, and your ability to perceive these differences could save your life or lead to an early death. So if you find yourself dealing with social friction that you believe is motivated by racism, try adjusting how you're dressed and see if you have the same result.

Racism is just a subset of out-group exclusion. Mimic the group that you're trying to break into with similar dress and you will notice that people will act warmer towards you. If you want to make a statement, wear the paragon version of their style of dress. Meaning the trendiest version of their style of clothing. Because clothing is an indicator of status, you will find it can be a lot easier to be the default leader of the group.

Brendon: Good fashion displays a number of different things but most importantly, especially when dealing with subcultures, if you want to control the frame you first have to fit in before you lead.

D: Race

William: We'll be frank; people interact with people from different races differently. People interact with people who have different accents differently, and you have to be aware of this so that you know how to either mitigate the potential deficit or utilize it as an advantage.

Brendon: It's important to understand that Bill and I are pointing out facts with no moral judgements about the rightness or wrongness of them. The fact is that depending on where you are in the world, and the social environment that surrounds you, simply being one "race" or another is going to affect your status and your ability to control frames.

Just understand that it *is* a factor in determining how you're going to control frame.

There are certain things that black people can say in America that white people can't say. At the same time, there are certain things that a black person can do in America that will bring about a level of social scrutiny that wouldn't happen if a white person did them; and it's critical to understand those nuances because they will affect the way that you control the frame socially and gain status.

It may not be right, but it's the way the world is at the moment.

William: What you want to keep in mind is that when people interact with you they make assumptions about you. Race is one of the characteristics people use to tell themselves a story about the person they are interacting with. Your race is nothing but a brand, a list of positive and negative attributes that we associate with that particular brand.

Absent other information we utilize stereotypes to paint a picture of the other person. What you want to do is be aware of the negative stereotypes associated with your race. Think about clothing and speech choices that will help the person you are interacting with make better assumptions. This will reduce the potential conversational deficit that you might experience because of your ethnic background.

Now some people reading this will be upset with that piece of advice, it sounds like what we are encouraging is to diminish your differences in order to assimilate. This is exactly what we are arguing in favor of. There will be times that being different will function as a handicap. Know when uniformity is rewarded and do what you can to blend in. Don't worry about doing something to stand out; your race is doing that for you.

There are also positive stereotypes that are part of the collective conscious, find out what those are as well, amplify them when appropriate. The rules of the game aren't the same for any two people; figure out what rules don't apply to you and your tribe.

If there's a positive stereotype that's associated with your race and it's an attribute you don't possess, don't correct people who make that assumption. Assumed competence is an easy way to have an implicit frame. For example, if people believe you're good at math, they are more likely to trust you when you make assertions about history even though the two have very little to do with each other. If situations come up to display this assumed skill, just hide behind disinterest rather than incompetence.

Brendon: We can see in the news, especially, a lot of frame control and jockeying for status that occurs around racial narratives in the United States right now, and it's important for you to understand this because that public frame battle *does* affect the way that you operate in the world. Go look at examples of how people who look like you are portrayed at their best and at their worst.

You don't have to internalize them but it is important that you're aware of them and that you can play into the good ones while avoiding the bad ones.

William: We want to make this clear, blaming someone's behavior towards you as just "racism" is lazy and will deprive you from finding other ways to get what you want. Deconstruct what other things it might be other than racism. This will allow you to have a champion frame instead of a victim frame in situations where you might have been discriminated against.

Dig deeper whenever you feel that race is the reason why you're not succeeding. How were you dressed? How was the sound of your voice? What was your level of familiarity? Were you qualified? Were you overqualified? How could you have approached the situation better? Is there someone of the same race as you who got the opportunity? What were the differences between you and them? What did people of a different race than you do differently to get that same opportunity?

Asking yourself a bunch of questions that are growth-focused and that will give you an internal locus of control in the situation. If you can find places to improve, you can make a new plan rather than sitting around frustrated. It cripples you to believe that the world should be fair, it's not, and never will be, now find out how to use the world's inherent unfairness to your advantage.

Remember, if someone does not like you and you want something they have, it's up to you to figure out how to get what you want.

E: Looks

William: Looks are an implicit form of status. Good looking people have to put less effort into being accepted, ugly people must put a lot. The better looking you are, the more opportunities will find you. Your looks are another social passport.

Good looking people have what is called "the halo effect," where people project positive attributes on the person. I would tell you that one of the best ways to have an implicit frame as a man is to work out and be muscular.

The more muscular and attractive you are the more likely other people will be to fall under your spell in conversation. That's why good-looking people tend to have strong frames, because they interact with the expectation of getting what they want.

For this reason, you also have to be aware of your own headspace when you're around attractive people. Make sure you are not supplicating without a strategic reason. Ask yourself, "Would I be doing this if I didn't find them so attractive?"

Brendon: Take some time to make sure you're healthy. One of the quotes that I'm very fond of comes from Arnold Schwarzenegger, he says, "Everything begins with the body and ends with the body."

Taking care of yourself is part of the foundation of having a good frame. The more fit you are, the clearer mind you're going to have, the better you dress, the better you look, the more accepting people are going to be of the frames that you are trying to control socially and the narratives you're trying to sell.

We're not trying to say that it's fair that good-looking people have an easier time winning and controlling frame, but it's just the way that it is. Now, just because you don't look like Zac Effron or Chris Pine or Idris Elba doesn't mean that you can't do something here. Everybody has it within their power to take care of themselves, get the proper amount of exercise, eat right, sleep right, and dress in a way that's flattering for their bodies.

F: Laws, Regulation, and Shame (Rearing Tools of Society)

William: The consequences of going against a macro-cultural frame can cost you everything. If you violate a law you can end in prison. Violating a regulation can become a massive inconvenience and doing a shameful act could result in you living in exile.

The fear of shame is one of the most powerful behavioral deterrents. Shame is the feeling that comes from breaking a cultural rule. Shame can come from things as small as getting caught picking your nose or as big as sexual misconduct.

Some people fear shame more than death. It's common knowledge that the biggest fear people have is public speaking. I asked myself about why this was the case and I came to the realization that if you spoke publicly and offended the wrong person in your tribe 30,000 years ago, they not only probably killed or exiled you but they probably did the same to your family too.

Shame is an incredibly powerful tool, and countless horrible atrocities and punishments have been done as a result of someone breaking the rules of society. That's why it is important to understand how to navigate the frames set by society with care because it is dangerous to violate them.

G: When & How to go Against Cultural Frames

William: In order to understand when to go against a cultural frame, first look for how regularly this rule is enforced, and who has the power or the energy to enforce this rule. Secondly, ask yourself what you stand to gain. If you come across a "rule" which has low levels of enforceability and no one who's anxious to enforce it, while the benefit of bending or breaking the rule could have massive benefit, go for it.

Brendon: Understand, this is why people are afraid to act socially: You know in your bones that if you violate social rules, very bad things could happen. You should remind yourself that we live in a time now in which violating some social rules are fine. But it's important to understand because we violate social rules, laws, regulations, and social morals at our own peril.

A contemporary example might be when an American college student recently visiting North Korea stole a sign and was sent to a death camp. There are stories of Australian tourists getting lifetime jail sentences for possessing just a small amount of recreational drugs for personal consumption in southeast Asia.

William: The concept of acceptability is always changing. A hundred years ago, Brendon and I collaborating on a book would've been seen as unacceptable in the American south because Brendon is white and I am black, but now these types of creative partnerships are the norm and are even encouraged.

The Power Bible

Remember that cultural rules create massive inefficiencies in the market. If you being a foreigner will allow you to take market share because domestic entrepreneurs cannot advance due to it being a taboo, take notice and take advantage, but only after you figure out what might be the consequence.

Always look for which way the social pendulum is swinging; where there is a change there is also unyielded treasure. If you do find a cause for which you are willing to risk your reputation for the potential reward, remember the adage, boldness wins when it does not vanish.

You cannot make an unpopular statement and then retreat when rebuked. You will look like a coward. When asked to repeat your position, do so proudly but without changing your stance to be more palatable or polemic.

If someone demands you clarify, state that you will do so only if they listen in earnest and do not interrupt. This allows the conversation to happen on your terms. You are controlling the frame because you are controlling the conditions for your response. This will also prevent you from having to defend a straw man position. Never apologize to a mob. The mob will demand to be fed an apology but what it's after is blood.

The worst part about apologizing to a mob is that it diminishes your ability to summon a counter mob. Cult followings are the benefit of standing up for what you believe. The more taboo, the more motivated the mob.

Brendon: Jordan B. Peterson's rise in the media is a great example.

William: Part of the reason why Jordan B. Peterson is such a compelling figure is that he didn't fold from social pressure. This captured people's attention who were already sympathetic to his viewpoint and those who were encouraged by his action.

How Jordan B. Peterson is able to withstand protest, media hit pieces, and threats on his life is by having a strong inner frame. He constructed his powerful frame by embodying his values.

H: Social Pressure

William: Social pressure is an inextricable part of the human experience. It is the implicit and explicit force that people, groups, and cultures apply on to individuals to make them act in a particular way.

It can be as harmless as a librarian asking you to keep your voice down or as destructive as the SS demanding you tell them where the Jews are hiding.

Social pressure is often masked by the word "awkward." When people say that you're making a situation awkward that is them using social pressure to get you to change your behavior. Now sometimes you're in the wrong, but there are times you are in the right.

It was awkward when Rosa Parks didn't give up her chair at the front of the bus, but her resistance to social pressure was a catalyst to the civil rights movement of the 50's and 60's. Do not be afraid of making things awkward to get what you want.

Do not be afraid of attention. The more you stand out and grow as an individual the more social pressure you will receive. So if you speak in a dominant way and have a strong frame, expect people to push back on you and say bad things about you in order to test whether you are strong enough to be the leader.

Celebrities must withstand an enormous amount of social pressure. Every word they say can be met with some level of criticism from the masses. People who are in managerial or public facing positions also face social pressure as they are responsible for firing and reprimanding people. Situations, where you apply social pressure onto others, will lead to you experiencing more yourself.

The people with the strongest inner frames are able to withstand lots of social pressure. Those with weak frames crumble under the pressure. Social pressure is made more intense when you take into consideration the apparent status and authority of the individual who's applying the pressure. The more powerful the person who criticizes, the more powerful the urge to comply.

The amount of people who are hostile towards you matters too. For example, if one person says "I hope you die" you might be able to shrug it off, but if one hundred thousand people are saying it, you might feel compelled to end it all.

Brendon: The amount of social pressure that you're going to be under only increases as you gain frame control in the world around you and become more dominant. As someone who is the progenitor of those frames gaining a foothold around you, and the biggest beneficiary, you're going to have a lot of social pressure to change your frame. You're going to be pushed on both by people who are in authority positions because your frames are now threatening theirs, and by simply more people who are now encountering your frame for the first time. Even though those people might not all be higher status, quantity has a quality all its own. So, as your frame gets stronger you're going to face more social pressure.

William: Feelings of guilt, public breakdowns, insomnia, self-harm, self-imposed exile, and in some cases, suicide are all feelings and behaviors that can manifest from having an overwhelming amount of social pressure applied on you. This is why you see celebrities have public breakdowns, shaving their heads, dealing with addiction, etc. They are weathering a never-ending storm of millions of people's opinions about their lives.

Brendon: What you have to get into is a practice of withstanding social pressure, and that needs to look like whatever it looks like for you. For me, it looks like a practice of reminding myself that other people can be wrong and ultimately, *I* know who I am, so I don't need to have other people tell me who I am. I even write these things to myself in a journal and read them back.

Especially in the Western world, we've entered a dark time in which a negative kind of social maneuver often takes place. There are going to be people who will try to tell you who you are because your identity to them is meaningful in one way or another. Now, this is them attempting to enforce frame over you through shame or anger, but what they're trying to do is get you to comply with them and destroy your frame.

William: You can actually fight that instinct by labeling the experience in your mind "No, I'm just feeling social pressure. None of this is real." Even if all the feelings in your body are telling you to do what you're told, don't listen, stand there and wait it out. You don't have to respond to anything people are saying about you or at you. Just take a deep breath and remind yourself that the feelings you're feeling are the result of social pressure and they will pass.

There are two reflexive actions that people have when social pressure is applied, fight or flight. In many cases both are wrong. Even though you don't want to comply or walk away, you also don't want to scream and yell. Both responses are two sides of the same coin, you lost your frame and everyone in the room knows. Instead, all you want to do is hold the position. We will talk about the specifics of this later on in the book, but we just want to say that you will feel social pressure and we want to put a name on that feeling.

So when you are testing your frame in the world, say to yourself, "Oh, I am feeling the instinct to buckle under social pressure. This is to be expected. I am going to hold strong." The awareness that this is expected will aid you as you try to apply our advice in your own life.

Environmental Frames

The Power Bible

V – Environmental Frames

A: Subcultures

William: Subcultures tend to have their own set of rules. Some of these rules are explicitly stated, like the "no smoking" sign inside a club, the others might be heavily implied, such as with rope barricades separating you from the DJ.

Brendon: Now, this is important to understand because you, reading this book, operate within subcultures that are both not named and have no explicit rules. However, they do exist. The subculture is real and so are the rules in that subculture. Once you understand what these rules are, you can "See the matrix," as everyone is fond of saying.

A good example of an unspoken rule at let's say, the Laugh Factory comedy club that Bill and I both do stand-up at, is if you're a patron, you don't continue a conversation over the comedian on stage. In the Laugh Factory, no one has made the rule that you must remain quiet explicit, it's just understood. If you were being loud and obnoxious, they would ask you to leave even though that rule was never made explicit at the time of entry.

Comedians are bound by the rules in that subculture as well. Each comedian has a certain amount of time that they're allotted on stage. The Laugh Factory has a little red light that only the comedian can see from the stage that signals it's about time to wind up their material and get off stage. If they run that light, meaning the comedian continues their performance rather than finishing, they will stop being invited back to the Laugh Factory because it's disruptive to the show.

The Laugh Factory has an agenda to have other comedians to perform on stage, it has to finish up the show, it has to get a new audience and then sell more tickets because that's how their business model works.

William: We want you to develop an acute awareness of etiquette. There is actual utility to etiquette, it's a social signaling mechanism that shows who belongs and who does not. Your understanding of these unspoken rules will allow people to trust that you belong; your ignorance of the rules will have invisible doors closed in your face.

For example, while my parents were living in London, they were regularly invited to Royal Family luncheons. My dad was relieved that my mom had attended finishing school and knew which utensil to use when. Not knowing the right fork to use wouldn't have been addressed at dinner but it would have been a signal that my mom didn't belong.

This might seem arbitrary but the benefit behind etiquette is that there are some things it would have required experience to know. This would have made it easy to spot imposters or people with a lack of experience. Etiquette did not arise for this purpose but those are inferences people make when a person does not follow the unstated rules.

Brendon: This absolutely occurs in the United States as well. I grew up between two different worlds in Detroit, one of country clubs and privilege and one of blue collar workers; I noticed that different etiquette distinguished the two classes. You can't show up to a five-course dinner at a country club in a dirty Carhartt work jacket. However, some of these rules of etiquette can actually be bent and broken by someone holding special status.

B: Power Dynamics

Brendon: As we talk about power dynamics, let's define power as the ability to affect meaningful change in the world. That may sound like a vague definition, but that's because power can look many different ways, but status is the social recognition of the power that someone is perceived to have, and that also can look many different ways.

Fixed power is also symbolic power; it recognizes that someone has already achieved a certain level of authority or power that is deferred to. A police officer is a good example of this because a police officer holds symbolic power. If there's a fight on the street but a police officer shows up, people will listen to the officer. The police officer has a symbol of power in the form of a badge, and they have the socially recognized ability to enforce the law with the use of violence. In fact, they have a mandate on that violence, given to them by the sovereign people. That's a fixed level of status and power, and the ability to use that power, the power of law.

Contextual status and fluid status are slightly different. Contextual status occurs within a social situation, but fluid status is from moment to moment to moment.

William: Power is intimately tied to status. Let's say you're out at a nightclub, the person who has fixed status at a nightclub is the nightclub owner. There is almost nothing that can happen throughout the night that's going to cause him to lose his status; he's going to be able to get free drinks from the bar, he's going to be able to enter all rooms and people will move out of the way when he enters the room.

Let's say that Brendon buys table service for the night. Brendon would have what we call "contextual status." Brendon has the status of being a guy standing at a table with drinks but if we violate the rules or when our table service runs out, he would lose his claim to status in the environment.

Then, there is fluid status. Now, fluid status is if Brendon and I instead of buying a table, we make friends with someone at the table. We have status as long as we remain in their good graces but if they tell us to leave, we lose our status, so our status is fluid.

The difference between static, contextual, and fluid status is how many privileges you are privy to in the environment, and how difficult it would be to remove those privileges. The owner of the club is pretty much omnipotent unless police, government regulators, or the bank shut him down. Even then, lawyers would get called, tons of paperwork would have to be filled out and court proceedings would have to take place before he could be ousted.

The person who buys the table for a night has a whole host of privileges that come with the table that they are entitled to. These perks are usually listed on different promotional material and menus. The significance of that is the person who has bought the table could point to the promotional material if he's not getting the services that were being advertised. That being said, if a person who has purchased table service is getting unruly or is difficult to deal with, an employee with authority, probably the manager or owner could kick them out.

Finally, there's me and Brendon, we have no symbolic agreement that entitles us to be at the table, and if the guy who bought the table decides we have overstayed our welcome, he can just ask the waiter to tell us to leave and we would have to go.

Power is the ability to enforce consequences. Status is your access to privilege based on your relationship to power. The more power you believe you have, the stronger your frame. Other people's awareness of your relationship to power is important.

For example, if a man in street clothes stops you and tells you to get down on your knees, you probably won't comply. But, if he says "I'm a police officer" and flashes a badge, you are a lot more likely to drop to your knees. This is because you are now aware of his relationship to power.

Brendon: People tend to default to the frames of those who have higher authority or power. The reason that people defer to a judge's decision is because it is enforced with the weight of the law. So, if a judge says you need to pay the plaintiff in a case $500 and you refuse to do it, the continued shirking of the law will result in more penalties for you until the time that you either go to jail and remain in jail and your life is changed forever or you accept and comply.

That's because all the social cues and frames relate to the power of the judge and none to you. However, in a different social situation with the judge, that same case might not be true, which is why status can sometimes be contextual. The fact that you are a judge and have lots of power in the world doesn't translate to a situation where you might be out skiing and dealing with a ski instructor. The instructor knows more about skiing and knows more about how someone should handle themselves on the ski slope than the judge does.

William: To highlight the transience of power even more, if that judge walks down the hall to a different courtroom she no longer has power. This highlights the most powerful distinction between how you should interact with people who are in a perceived superior position. Do not defer to people based on status but based on their relationship to power.

For example, let's say you're in a conversation with someone and John Travolta shows up and ask you if you could grab him a cup of water. You don't have to get him water even though you might feel a strong impulse to comply. That instinct to comply is rooted in the fact that status used to be intimately tied with power in primordial times, but that is no longer the case.

John Travolta has celebrity status, which means he enjoys a lot of privileges that you might not have access to, but he does not have power over you. Remember, power is a privilege but not all privileges give you power.

Brendon: That's a great explanation.

William: We live in a status ambiguous culture where billionaires wear T-shirts to meetings, while there are people, who because of the credit card culture are wearing $5000 suits but have no money in the bank.

A lot of people say there are easy ways to distinguish who has power and who doesn't. Some say look for the best-dressed person in the room, but in most upscale restaurants the best-dressed person is the waiter. Hyper-conformity is evidence of a lack of status and power. It sub-communicates that you do not have enough status to break the rules.

So instead of looking for something that is a definite indicator of status, you want to train your eyes to look for irregularities in behavior. In both the person you are looking at and the people reacting to them. Is the person being left alone? Or is everyone coming up and talking to them? Both of these could be examples of someone having status and power.

One clear way you can see if someone has power is by how many "rules" they are breaking and yet are they being accepted despite this. The bigger the taboo, the more status you signal if you're still accepted.

Brendon: It's because people who tend to have status tend to break rapport more often because they don't care as much about maintaining it.

C: Relevant and Irrelevant Rules

William: There are multiple factors that you must look at when you hear about rules. The first question you must ask yourself is "who enforces this rule?" if the person who enforces this rule does not have a lot of power themselves, it might be worth testing the rule to see what the result of transgressing it is.

Another question you want to ask is "how often is this rule enforced?" A rule that's clearly stated but never enforced is an opportunity for you to take a short cut.

For example, Ivy League schools do not accept bribes to get students in. This is looked at as academic dishonesty. They do, on the other hand, take "donations" that they "consider" when looking at your child's application. This is a rule that is relevant but if you know how to present the behavior in a different way, it does not apply.

The same thing is true when there's a line outside a nightclub that's long. I know that I don't have to stand in line to get into the club. I know there are tons of spaces available in the club and I know partially that the reason they have a line outside is to give the illusion that it's going to be a fun night. So, I go up to the bouncer and I say "hey, can you let me and my friends in?" and I give him $100, now I get to cut the line. The line was an irrelevant rule and I understood that and I got into the club hours earlier because of my understanding of that rule.

Brendon: This is a good example of why you want people to filter into your frame rather than necessarily accepting their frames. So, the win-

win of this situation is that the bouncer just made $100 and you guys got into the club faster. Now, that's not the way the rules are explicitly supposed to work, but you created a new reality by enforcing your frame on a situation, and that reality was beneficial to everyone... except the people waiting in line.

D: Rapid Ascension Strategies

William: This brings us to rapid ascension strategies. In any subculture, there is what's called a dominance hierarchy. A dominance hierarchy can be defined as a type of social hierarchy that arises when members of a social group interact, to create a ranking system where members are likely to compete for access to limited resources and mating opportunities.

These hierarchies are everywhere and their stratification is rooted in either competence, alliances, familiarity, or trade. Let's say this, in MMA, if you are a highly skilled fighter, let's say Conor McGregor, you are at or near the top of the dominance hierarchy in MMA. In fact, you cannot be at the top of the dominance hierarchy in MMA without being a highly skilled fighter.

This comes from the fact that there are objective ways to determine who is competent and who is not. A person who is competent at fighting is able to defeat his opponent in the octagon. Although wins might be contested, it is often fairly obvious who won the fight and who didn't.

The more objective the standards are, the more likely the dominance hierarchy is to be organized by competence. There's no way for us to lie, either you got in the ring and knocked out the guy or you got knocked out, either you took more punches or landed more punches. Your goal in competence hierarchies is unambiguous. Your goal in MMA is to win the fight, either by KO, TKO or by the judge's decision.

Competence hierarchies are not limited to sports. In fact, most subdomains have competence as an organizing factor to some degree.

Stand up comedy, for instance, is an art form where you cannot ascend without being competent. With standup, the goal is to make the audience laugh, and if there is an absence of laughter when the comedian is on stage everyone is aware. Not all art forms can be judged with an objective lens, that's why most art subdomains are ruled by what we call an alliance hierarchy.

In the art world, your alliances with galleries, other artists, celebrities, and museums are what help you ascend. Sure, competence is a barrier to entry to be relevant but it's not an organizing force at the top of the hierarchy.

In art "You're as powerful as your network," if you talk to the right people and they like you enough to expose you to their audience, you ascend. It's not about paying your dues, it's about finding patrons who will make other people believe you have.

Brendon: I think that's completely true, that the alliances are the ones that work off of mutual benefit. So, just to return to this idea of paying the bouncer to let you into the club for $100, it could be a number of different ways that that value is exchanged but you create a new reality that is mutually beneficial for both of you. The same thing is true with forging alliances; they occur because someone wants to see you rise because it benefits them.

William: Exactly. And you made them think that it benefits them.

Brendon: You've created a frame in which your success equals value for them.

William: Next, we will discuss the role familiarity has in ascension. Ascension based on familiarity is different than ascension rooted in competency and alliances, namely because familiarity is to get your foot in the door, where competence and alliances are what will take you to the top.

I'll start with a story about when I first moved to New York. When I arrived in New York after living in Chicago, I didn't have too many connections in the New York comedy scene. So I decided that I was going to spend 3 hours a day at our friend James Altucher's club, Standup New York.

At first, no one would acknowledge me. I just sat in the bar next to famous comedians like Tracy Morgan, Judah Friedlander, and Godfrey, just waving hi and bye. But over time people started to see me around and believed that I was on the show, I wasn't, but this belief made comedians open up to me. Soon I was asked to perform, asked to be on big podcasts, and became more integrated into the New York stand up ecosystem.

A lot of the opportunities I got were just from being a familiar face. I didn't say much, but I did make sure not to say something stupid. I was aware when I was bothering someone and would pull back. Slowly even the coldest of comics would begin to open up.

I didn't have to be competent at stand-up comedy and I didn't have to necessarily build a strong alliance for them to showcase me, I just had to not mess up. A lot of times, especially when you try to get in the door at a place, people try to make up for lost ground all at once. They try to be overly friendly and in your face, asking for opportunities on the first or second meeting. This can work but often times the advance is rejected because you don't have enough social capital for them to want to give you what you want.

Brendon: Returning to the concept of subcultures; subcultures have rules. Some of those rules are explicit, many of them are implicit and unspoken, but when people gain familiarity with you, seeing you in the same location with a consistent demeanor, this shows those who observe you that you've passed the rules. It shows you belong.

William: One of the benefits of becoming familiar with both people and your surroundings is that you will learn which stated rules don't matter and what unstated ones do. Also the more time you spend in a particular location, the easier it will be for you to have a strong frame because your level of comfort will increase. For example, if someone offends you at your house, it's a lot easier for you to stand up for yourself than if someone offends you in the lobby right before an interview.

Another way to rise to the top of a hierarchy is to trade something of value. A great example of this is the Conor McGregor v. Floyd Mayweather fight. McGregor was able to fight the world champion undefeated boxer, Floyd Mayweather, with having zero professional boxing fights under his belt. The reason McGregor was able to do that was because he was able to offer an extraordinary value of the pay per views purchases that McGregor fans would make. So, even though he wasn't at the top of the boxing dominance hierarchy, he had enough value that he had built up in his own subculture that he could translate that to having a $400 million fight with Floyd Mayweather.

Brendon: This worked because he was at the top of his own hierarchy and was able to leverage his status within the M.M.A. hierarchy for a fight even though the boxing hierarchy is much larger and higher. He moved from the top of one hierarchy to another.

William: These types of exchanges can take different forms. So, let's say that I want a place at a university and I didn't make good enough scores to get a scholarship, I can offer that value to be at those classes by paying full price for the university. I'm offering the value of money to get the opportunity. Sometimes the value is what skills you can offer the person. This does not mean become a sycophant, however.

A person who ends up being a sycophant is someone who does non-skilled work in order to receive attention from the desired individual. Because the work is not specialized the skilled person will likely not respect you. As we stated earlier, respect is garnered from the perceived difficulty of an action. Something like getting a coffee isn't perceived as being difficult, so no matter how many times you do it, it won't increase the amount of respect they have for you.

Now the exception for this is if they make you do a menial task, such as grab coffee, but they are also sharing with you specialized insight. But as quickly as possible you want to assist them on something they acknowledged as being difficult so their esteem for you will grow over time.

The Power Bible

Brendon: Offering a powerful person something they can't do is the best way to try to gain powerful alliances and ascend into hierarchies quickly.

The bottom line is this: when it comes to frame control, power dynamics are real and they are relevant. Once you have an understanding of status, dominance hierarchies, and how to forge alliances within and between them, you will be able to strategize these tactics in concert and help you achieve your goals quickly.

Frame Control

The Power Bible

VI – Frame Control

Introduction To Frame Control

Brendon: For most of this book, we've mentioned frames. We've talked about how to gain a strong inner frame over yourself, and mentioned how frames from the world affect you and the way you perceive your life. Now, we'll discuss directly how to control frames socially, and the things that affect your ability to control frames.

A: What is Frame Control?

William: Once again, a frame is the context through which a person, situation, or conversation is perceived. Frame control is your ability to control how the person, situation, or conversation is perceived. Put more simply, frame control is the art of controlling perception. I'll give you an example.

Let's say that Brendon and I were walking down the street and we see a shooting, and someone is killed. Afterward, a police officer asks us, "What happened?" I say, "That guy murdered him," Brendon says, "no the guy was defending himself."

Now, only one of those narratives can actually exist. If my frame wins, the murderer could spend the rest of his life behind bars. If Brendon's frame wins, the man who was in a struggle for his life gets to continue to live as a free man.

Brendon: How do you perceive yourself? Do you feel that you have value to offer other people? Do you feel you can make a meaningful contribution? All of these things are frames. Frames are how your brain contextualizes and interprets data from the world around you.

William: Frames exist in the mind but have tangible consequences. This is because we live in a socially constructed reality. This means that most of our reality, our relationships, laws, and institutions, must be recognized and accepted by others in order to function.

If you say you are in a romantic relationship with someone, that statement only has value if they agree. If you want to call that person "my wife," both she and the state have to recognize and accept the label. Some titles only have a few conditions that need to be met to be bestowed, while others require a lot of conditions that need to be performed in a particular order to be recognized by the community.

For example, the $20 bill in my pocket only has value because people accept that it has value, but in order for the $20 bill to have value, it must go through a specific ritual in order to be recognized universally. If it only has the appearances of a $20 bill but was made in a warehouse instead of the Federal Reserve, then once someone with the authority and ability to tell that the $20 is not authentic, it will no longer be accepted.

In this way, the world operates like a massive role-playing game, with each person playing multiple roles. Some titles are self-bestowed, others are a reward or punishment from the community. The roles we assume affect how we interact with each others' frame and even our own frame.

Brendon: The $20 bill example is a good one because it actually only has value for what it's exchanged for, and that value is a social agreement. In the same fashion, frames are also a kind of social agreement, but many of them happen on a level that occurs outside of conscious awareness, before someone actually thinks about what they're agreeing to.

Frame control is using tools in social interactions to influence the context of what's happening, and just like in the $20 bill example, a $20 bill can have a lot of purchasing power if you convince someone that the thing you're buying from them is actually worthless.

William: Everything that exists socially, from the price of things to the enforcement of laws are just frames given by an institution or person that has authority. The more "important" the entity, the stronger the frame. Me telling Brendon, "Hey, I don't want to get lunch there" is different than the government saying "you cannot have lunch here because they did not meet their sanitation requirements." In fact, accepting a frame is *granting* authority to the giver of the frame.

Brendon: That's a great point.

William: I put the word "important" in quotes to emphasize that importance is often an illusion. Rules are not as intractable as we are led to believe. There are rewards for those who know how to bend the rules and punishments for those who break them. That is how there are companies that make hundreds of billions of dollars a year but somehow pay less in taxes than you and I. The companies that pay nothing in taxes get away with it because they hire people who know the rules and how to bend them. Meanwhile, if you just stopped paying taxes, you would be breaking the rules and it would only be a matter of time until you were fined or imprisoned.

That being said, there are rules that matter and rules that don't. The rules that don't matter but you tacitly obey are the equivalent of you locking yourself in a social prison.

Brendon: These kinds of rules are why you might be afraid to approach an attractive person that you want to talk to, get the job you *really* want, or even be the person you feel deep down.

B: Why is "Frame Control" Important?

William: Frame control is important because much of what we get in life is the result of how well we do in the conversations that matter.

The sad thing is, usually the higher the stakes of the conversation, the more likely you are to lose control of the frame. So, frame control is important because it can be the reason why you make your first million or the reason why your marriage ends in divorce.

Brendon: How well you control frame can be the reason why you go to jail, and it can be the reason why you become President of the United States.

C: Vocal Control

William: Human beings express and communicate emotions through tone and volume. As we mentioned in the chapter on conditioning, mammals have used tone and volume to communicate with each other for hundreds of millions of years.

Your ability to control your voice is paramount to getting people in the emotional state to buy into your frame. Most people's frames come out of their emotional disposition at the given moment. Your ability to give them a feeling is as close as you can get to compelling them to act.

Your tone of voice sub-communicates your level of confidence, your mood and at times, your true intention. A frame hack is to learn how to speak with certainty even when you are filled with doubt. The techniques we teach later on in the book will have a muted effect unless you have a firm grasp of your tone and volume in those situations.

Although we will go into this in far greater depth in our courses and coaching, one thing you want to be aware of is when you are taking a submissive tone. A submissive tone is a tone that sounds like you are constantly asking questions, even if you are making a statement. Meaning that your voice goes up in pitch at the end.

Certain accents are more submissive than others. For example, people who have Indian accents often sound submissive even if they are in positions of authority because of this upward pitch at the end of their sentences. What you want to do is be able to speak in a way where your voice has a downward inflection at the end of the sentence, as if you're talking to the floor.

Another thing to be conscious of is that the lower you perceive your status in the environment, the harder it will be for you to speak loudly and with authority. So before situations where you know that might be nervous, go to a secluded area and do voice exercises to make sure you don't sabotage yourself in conversation.

With body language, remember to look as expansive and comfortable as socially acceptable for that particular context. If you remember these two things you will effortlessly look like the highest status person in the room from a body language standpoint.

D: How to Know When You're in Someone's Frame

Brendon: The way that you know that you're in someone else's frame is if you find yourself reacting by experiencing a lot of emotions. That's the simplest way to know.

Experiencing lots of emotion indicates that you're within someone else's frame.

We've talked before earlier in the book about being in someone else's frame. It's not wrong to be within someone else's frame; when a police officer shows up and takes control of a social situation and tells you to comply, it isn't wrong to do it.

I was in the rally to restore sanity in Washington D.C. in 2010. There were hundreds and hundreds and thousands of people in the National Mall in Washington D.C. and in order to see the stage I had to climb a tree. Now, what I did not know was that climbing the trees in the National Mall in Washington is illegal; there's no sign that says that it's illegal but it is. There were too many people for the police to be able to arrest everyone but as people exited the National Mall after the event ended, I was still up in the tree when a group of police officers walked over and pointed guns at me and my friends who were in the tree with me.

They leveled M16s at us, pointed at us, and yelled in a very loud voice, "get down, get down from the tree right now!" I jumped down from the branches immediately. The police officers told me to get on my knees, put my hands behind my head, pull my hands out of my pockets and comply with everything they said. I was reacting to them because they had the stronger frame and I was within their frame, I was experiencing a lot of emotion, as you can imagine, with a loaded gun pointed at me. I knew I hadn't done anything wrong but I was scared and I was following what they were saying.

That's why I know that I'm in someone else's frame. If I'm on a sales call, someone says something very direct to me like, "we're probably not going to do business together," if I start reacting to it then I know that I'm within their frame. And that's not where I want to be. You have to cultivate an attitude of understanding that when you're experiencing emotions, it indicates you have attachments to things working a certain particular kind of way and that is within someone else's frame.

You can feel this when it happens and you've probably felt it throughout your life, you don't always know exactly how it happens but you can feel when it does happen.

William: Generally speaking when you're in someone else's frame you will feel more emotionally volatile. This could be that a small act of disapproval makes you feel small or offended and action of approval makes you feel proud and happy.

If you have anxiety before your interaction with a person, it's much more likely that you will assume their frame because at that moment you have a weak inner-frame. If you leave a conversation, and have a lot of anxiety about how it went, it's likely that you were in their frame as well.

If you find yourself rushing to answer their questions or trying to think of the answer that they want you to give, that's evidence of you being in their frame. If you accept commands without thinking you're in their frame. If when you both speak at the same time and you reflexively, stop talking, you're in their frame. If you're very aware of how much of their time you are taking up and you are rushing to make your points, you are in their frame. If you are constantly using disqualifiers, such as, "it's just," "I'm sorry," "no big deal," etc. you're likely in their frame.

The Power Bible

Notice that a lot of these sounds like you're just being polite, but that's the thing about general etiquette: it is to avoid conflict. Sometimes getting what you want requires a level of confrontation and rather than teach people how to be socially dexterous we've taught them to be supplicative to avoid conflict.

Other behaviors to be cognizant of are you sitting in a way to take up as little space as possible, you're likely in their frame. If you feel the impulse to not talk loudly when you speak or have your voice crack during a conversation, you're in their frame.

Also if you spend a lot of time thinking about whether or not you should say something, that thought loop is evidence that you're in their frame because it comes from a place of being afraid of what the person's response would be, rather than assuming everything you say has value because you are saying it.

There is a degree component to this as well, meaning that there are levels to how deep you are in someone else's frame. For example, in Brendon's incident with the police he was deeply in their frame, so much so that without hesitation he dropped to the ground and got on his knees. This is very different than a friend of yours leading the conversation and asking you to do them a favor and you do it without question.

What you must be aware of is firstly, how many things you are doing to appease the person you are speaking with. Secondly, you must be aware of how far you will be willing to go to appease this person. When you start getting close to this limit, pause and gather your composure. When you are acting in someone's frame you might feel strong impulses to continue a course of action that might not be to your benefit. Understand that your impulse is just a biological shortcut to keep you safe and not evidence that they are instructing you to do something that would be to your benefit.

Get in the habit of asking yourself two questions in any conversation:

"Am I in their frame?

"Am I comfortable with being in their frame?"

If you ask these questions regularly you will be difficult to manipulate.

Brendon: You need to be very careful, especially in business to avoid situations that don't give you the opportunity to reflect.

Years ago, a very close friend of mine joined an insurance company as a salesman and they made him set up consultations with all of his friends and family. He talked me into coming in and I thought, "why not? I'll come in and do this and support my friend in his new job position." What happened was that I went into a very small room with him and his boss and another person and we sat down together and had this very pointed conversation about insurance; my insurance, my car insurance and how I was putting myself at risk and how my friend did a very good job by bringing me to the office to help point out to me exactly what I was doing wrong with my insurance.

They drew diagrams on a white board in the room and explained things to me about why my insurance was wrong and how I was putting myself at risk at every moment and wanted me to sign over my insurance to their company to protect myself that very minute. I couldn't do it, and didn't want to at the time anyway, but also couldn't do it and told them so. But the entire situation was designed to try and control the frame around me as much as possible to make it emotionally difficult for me to say no. And that's what frames do, they cause emotions in the people who are caught within them. If I had signed over, it would have been bad and that would have been a big problem that I would probably still be dealing with it to this day, but I didn't. However, those types of situations; high-pressure sales tactics, individuals trying to pressure you in one way or another, is something you definitely want to avoid.

These days I have a rule for myself to avoid making mistakes in high-pressure sales situations. I always say "no" to anything that requires me to do it right then, at the moment. I don't mind telling a salesperson "I have a rule that I have to wait 24 hours before I commit to doing anything." If they have a problem with that then the answer is always "no."

The Power Bible

William: So just asking those two questions periodically during the conversation will help you stay in control of the situation and will also have the auxiliary effect of making you more contemplative. Having a reflective demeanor will actually help you take back frame in many situations; we'll discuss more on that later.

When someone asks you a question, they are asserting their frame on you. This is not a bad thing. We aren't saying that you should stop answering questions, but we are bringing your awareness to that being an option.

The power of a question is in whether you choose to answer it. The second you reject a question you grab the frame at that moment. Now this should be used sparingly but it's an easy way to communicate that you're in control of the conversation.

There are also two types of personalities that ask questions, those who are interested in finding out about you and those who are interrogating you. The difference is that a person who's interested in finding out about you will be asking questions in a way that flatters you, and probably have no nefarious underlying intentions. A person who is interrogating you is looking for weakness. Weaknesses in your story or weaknesses in your character or both.

An interrogator will tend to ask questions in rapid succession. Focusing on particular details. You'll notice their tone will be short and authoritative, even if they have a smile. They will give non-verbal and sometimes verbal signals that they don't believe what you're saying. They will frame your responses in an unflattering light.

When being interrogated you should immediately stop answering questions. This is because the state that it puts you in will make you answer the question in a way that will likely not be to your benefit. You don't need to address their tone, just an "I'm not answering that" with silence and strong eye contact will usually cause them to retreat back to a more amiable disposition.

How To Take Back
Frame

The Power Bible

E: How to Take Back Frame

1. Label

William: Labelling is repeating what the person is proposing in a way that changes their position. Once they agree with your new description of what they you just said, you control the frame. The reason for this is by altering what they have stated, you have set a new standard for the conversation. If they asked you a question, you can yourself the question you actually want to answer, which will frame discussion in a different light. If you notice whenever politicians are being asked questions, they tend to repeat the question but they'll change it subtly.

Let's say an interviewer is asking you a question and maybe they're saying, "Hey, there are some gaps here on your resume, can you explain why?" and you repeat back to him "oh, so you're asking what I was doing from 2007 to 2010?" Now, this is subtly different; one of them is "give me the reason why you weren't working for a period of time," the other one is "hey, this is what I was doing in this period of time."

One frames the answer as an explanation; the other frames the answer as a narrative about those three years. One is time spent unemployed, the other could be a narrative of triumph and adventure.

Brendon: The times that I've used labeling in sales have been mostly to shift someone's perspective slightly by changing the vocabulary they're using. So, a prospect might say "Look, we're not looking for an e-mail service provider," and I might say in response "Well, you're probably not looking for an e-mail service provider but you probably *are* looking for a customer engagement platform." For the two terms, it doesn't matter what either of them are, it only matters that you're removing the associations with the terms by changing them and therefore changing the frame. These are just a bunch of different words that actually don't mean anything, it doesn't change what actually happened but the presentation of it does change the perception of it.

This definitely happens in politics because politicians change terms to make their plans and ideas sound more palatable. Everyone knows "look, I'm not pro-abortion, I'm pro-choice. I'm not against a woman's right to choose, I'm pro-life." These are really the same things; the position on the issue hasn't changed. I had a friend who changed his entire political beliefs once because he was talking with someone and they said, "are you a Republican or a conservative?" and he said "no" and they said "well, what do you believe in?" and he said "look, I think people should have the right to decide the things they do in their own lives and I think that nobody should tell them what to do and if they want to smoke weed, they should and if they don't want to pay a bunch of taxes, then they shouldn't have to do that." The person they were speaking to said, "OK, well, you're actually libertarian then" and to this day, that changed the way that my friend perceives himself politically. Just applying that label changed his entire outlook.

William: Labelling is a tactic used as an offensive strategy in a derogatory sense. So, you see a lot of times in the political climate where maybe somebody says something and the retort is that they are racist or that they're a communist. Now, the power of this is if they choose to respond to what you've just said, they are implicitly saying that there is enough evidence for them to attempt to disprove this label.

Brendon: It's important for someone reading this book to understand this: If someone even denies the label, they're complicitly agreeing with its usage. So, if someone says to me, "Brendon, you are racist" and I say "look, I'm not a racist, I have plenty of black friends," I'm already giving more support to their frame because I'm responding to it.

William: This is the section on how to take back frame. So, if somebody tries to label you, the thing to do in those circumstances is "If you really think that's who I am, I'm not carrying on this conversation"

Brendon: Or you can label them back. Ben Shapiro is a big proponent of this. If someone said to me, "Brendon, you're a racist" I'd say, "You're an idiot" or "You're just throwing slurs around."

William: But this can frequently end in a name-calling exchange, so once you label, if they want to continue to come at you, say "I'm not going to continue this conversation" and remove yourself.

Brendon: And then, especially in that circumstance, if someone is calling you a racist then you've already lost finding common ground with this person.

William: And that's actually a really powerful line, and that's what you should say. "You throwing that word around or trying to label me in this light shows that there's no longer an attempt to find common ground in this situation and I have to remove myself."

Brendon: Exactly, "I only engage with someone who's a partner in good faith. You're not, so I'm removing myself." It is great because the example that Bill just gave illustrates perfectly how to respond to this.

Basically, it's important to your own frame. In order to live a life of self-esteem and self-respect, you have to be in control of your own frame and you can make decisions on whose frames you decide to assent to or reject. If you choose to accept and believe those frames around you and respond to them, that *can* be fine, but if you don't have any control over any of them then you really don't have any kind of life at all.

William: Whoever's labelling the object of the conversation has control of the frame. You have created the foundation of the conversation which other people will use as a launching pad for their ideas.

Brendon: Whoever is the one who's giving the label is the one who controls the frame in conversation. The fact that Trump used 'fake news' and that has become the dominant term to describe a certain variety of reporting in the media shows that Trump is controlling the conversation.

William: Calling the news "fake news," is attacking the purpose of the news, which is to be a credible source for information.

Brendon: The same thing is true with his labelling of his opponents: "crooked Hillary," or "lying Ted." The fact that his opponents respond to those labels is proof that those labels stick and they're working.

William: Once again, one of the things that we're going to bring up over and over again is rhetoric beats logic most of the time. The bigger the audience, the more likely rhetoric will be to be a better tool of influence. Rhetoric and repetition is what sticks; a brand is built through repetition. So, what Trump did was he built a brand of insults that stuck on his opponents because he kept using them. Imagine if Nike changed its logo every day, the logo would be worthless. That's what Hillary's campaign did with Trump. One day he was a racist. One day he was a sexist. The next day he was a crook. He might be all these things but part of building a brand is focusing in on one thing and amplifying that.

Scott Adam actually talked about this in his book, *Win Bigly,* which was that Hillary started winning again when she kept repeating 'do you want his finger on the button?' All of a sudden, Trump's numbers started going a lot farther down. But then, when the 'grab them by the pussy' leak happened, they completely made a shift away from 'do you want his finger on the button?' and Scott Adam believes that might have been one of the reasons why she lost.

2. Ignore

William: In this section, we will discuss how to use selective silence to develop a power shift in a conversation.

I want you to imagine you are talking to someone and you ask them a question. They look at you so you know they heard it, but then they both don't answer and return to what they were doing. You feel embarrassed and want to save face so you ask the question again, this time they do not acknowledge you at all, carrying on. You would probably feel a mixed bag of emotions. Anger, anxiety, inferiority, but one thing you're not feeling is powerful. That's the power of selective silence. The person who has ignored you has created a validation vacuum.

In a validation vacuum it is difficult to remain confident. As many times we depend on people validating us to know that we have value.

The Power Bible

The more validation we receive the easier it is to feel confident in the moment. Many times when we perceive as someone being confident it's because they're receiving validation at the moment we're observing them. To see the true confidence a person has, withdraw your validation and see what happens.

You see this happen in stand-up comedy when a comedian is bombing. When a comedian bombs, they're getting feedback from the audience that what they're doing is bad. If it happens to you, you end up feeling drained. That's why people say that you can tell a great comedian by the way they bomb, because they have enough confidence to maintain their frame with no external validation.

Brendon: The fact that you don't need the audience's approval shows that you're selectively ignoring and you're having fun. Your act of selectively ignoring their response to you shows your superiority to them and then they can buy into your frame again. Essentially, you're breaking rapport with the audience.

Let's step back for a moment and remind ourselves that frames and the enforcing of frames are the way that human beings perceive hierarchical authority and status. And one of the ways that very high-status people remain high status is by ignoring the attempts to gain frame over them by people who are lower in status than they are.

So, for example, if let's say, Peter Thiel or Bill Gates or Donald Trump or some other type of high-status individual were accosted by someone on the street as they were getting out of a limousine, yelling insults at them. If they responded it would be lowering their status because the person who is yelling at them from the street is nowhere even near as high status as they are. And part of the reason I want to draw this to your attention is that ignoring someone else's attempt to outframe you does two things: First, it displays what looks typically like high-status behaviour, so if someone attempts to outframe you and you just ignore them outright, that's the same thing a high-status person would do. So, whether or not you are high status, you look high status. And second, what is important to understand, is that frames exist *because people put energy into them.*

So, the reason that 'crooked Hillary' stuck and the reason that 'fake news' sticks is because people continue to respond to the frame and that continues to fuel it. The more energy that people put into a frame, the more it exists, the more power it has, the more people respond to it. However, if you don't respond to it and you don't give energy to it, it dies. So by selectively ignoring it, you also let the attempt to outframe you die on the vine.

One of the ways, just like Bill, I discovered this was at a party. A very annoying girl was trying to status-frame me. I wasn't the most popular kid in general and I wasn't the most popular kid at this party specifically, but I was becoming more popular and of higher status socially and that threatened her, so she tried to status-frame me. I don't really even remember what she did, but I recall that when she was trying to status-frame me she tried to point out how awkward it was that I was at this party. Instead of responding to her, I rolled my eyes at her and turned around and spoke to someone else. As soon as I did that, I could feel a shift in my energy and her energy. Again, frames are mostly felt. For the rest of the party and for the rest of the evening she attempted to gain my attention back and every time I ignored her. Each time I could feel her try harder. So, this is very important to understand because if Hillary Clinton had wanted to properly respond to Donald Trump, she would not have responded to him at all, she would have continued banging the drum that he was an unsafe person to have near the nuclear button and it would have worked. But the problem was that she reacted to his frame, changed the things she was doing, and that continued to feed his frame.

William: When you ignore someone they typically have one of two emotional responses, anger or anxiety. Both of those emotional states make their frame weaker. Anger will make them look belligerent and easier to deceive and anxiety will make them meeker and more willing to accept your terms.

That being said, tools are context specific. This is why we say that you need to be selective with when and how you ignore people. Ignoring is a tool, but used too often and you come across as passive-aggressive, use it on the wrong person and you will look like an insubordinate fool.

Brendon: It's also important to point out that the ability to ignore does not just take place outside of yourself, it also takes place within yourself. In order to build a strong inner frame, you have to ignore feelings you have that disconfirm your strong inner frame. You might feel like you want to change your life, so you decide "I'm going to get up and I'm going to go running every morning," then you need to ignore feelings of tiredness, you need to ignore feelings of maybe "running is not for me," maybe "I'm not the kind of guy who can get in shape," maybe you feel scared because you're confronting personal limits. You need to ignore those feelings and focus only on the completion of your goal. That is how you build a stronger frame.

People don't talk enough about how to build a strong, confident inner frame but this is how you do it. Labelling works even more effectively when you're doing it on your own thoughts and feelings and emotions.

I used to be a very unathletic, chubby kid. I never did anything athletic, I never exercised very much. And when I was 16 years old, I decided through a lot of peer pressure, basically, to join the wrestling team in my high school. I tried to drop out a couple of times, like I said, I wasn't athletic; I tried to stop wrestling but through peer pressure, I eventually felt too self-conscious to drop out and stayed on the team. But I heard something that changed my life and changed the way that I look at exercise and the way that I look at the pain of exercise. A friend gave me a quote and it opened my eyes, his name was Richard Demsick, and he said, "pain is weakness leaving the body." After I heard that, from then on, any time I felt pain when I was exercising I reminded myself this is just my weakness leaving me and that labelling reframed the entire experience of working out.

Previously, that experience had been discomfort, pain, and pain indicated that something was wrong, that I needed to stop, that things were not OK. But after that point, pain indicated "this is where I should be. This is where I need to be. this is the space that I have to exist in order to become less weak and more strong." From then on I continued to exercise regularly, even joining mixed martial arts, cage fighting,

Crossfit, running marathons, and any other type of challenging physical activity. David Goggin, the author, says the same thing when he has talked about reframing himself into a powerful warrior.

William: David Goggins actually labelled himself. He got rid of "David Goggins" and made "Goggins." David Goggins was the man who was close to 300 pounds and couldn't run a mile. Goggins is one of the most accomplished ultramarathoners and elite athletes in the world as well as being a Navy SEAL and Army Ranger.

Brendon: Eminem did the same thing because when Eminem, Marshall Mathers, was originally rapping, he wrote rhymes in one way. However, he could not seem to get popular enough, he wasn't writing on things that were deep enough or resonated with people enough. Someone challenged him to write rhymes from his darker self and he created "Slim Shady." He wrote from that persona and it's not a coincidence that that his first breakout hit was "*I'm Slim Shady,*" because all of the things that he had rapped about up until that point just didn't resonate, but after that point, he wrote from a very aggressive, dark place and people really resonated with it.

3. Humor

William: When you laugh, it's an indicator that you're in somebody else's frame. Which is why if you get a person laughing when they're mad, they will be much more likely to listen to you.

Humor is what I call a high-risk high reward way of getting back the frame. The reason why it's high risk is because it's harder to be charismatic enough to be funny when you aren't leading the conversation. Depending on how deeply you are inside someone else's frame you might feel anxious which could potentially make you deliver the joke in a way that doesn't get a laugh.

Also when a person has the frame in the conversation, they're less likely to find things you say funny. Think about a scene in a movie where the protagonist tries to crack a joke to make the popular kids like them and they don't laugh. Another reason why using humor is high risk when you don't have frame is that if the joke falls flat, it can make you look even more socially incompetent which might push you deeper in their frame.

Brendon: Yeah, that's only every time I've been on stage! So, the reason humor is very powerful is that it shows that you're able to manage tension in a pleasant way and this indicates very strong leadership qualities. Because people can only be humorous, can only make jokes when they don't feel a lot of stress or tension, because if there is a lot of stress and tension, then someone has lots of attachments. It's very difficult to be humorous when you have attachments because you're not far enough away from the object to be able to shift your perspective on it. You know, no one is humorous when somebody is pointing a gun in their face and that's why screenwriters write characters who crack jokes at gunpoint in movies because it's interesting to watch. As someone who's had a gun pointed at him before, I can tell you I've never felt less funny than when a gun was pointed at my face. But the reason humor is so powerful is because you're actually manipulating someone else's emotions in the moment. It's a very visceral experience. As soon as someone feels the humor and laughs with you, it denotes frame acceptance because it provides such powerful relief. No one can laugh and be angry at the same time, it's impossible.

William: I mean, we've been paid to do stand-up comedy and then not been able to make people laugh, which is the only reason why they paid us.

Brendon: It's actually the worst feeling.

William: Yeah, you can't make people laugh who don't want to laugh.

Brendon: If you make people who are angry at you laugh at you then you have the keys to any kingdom - to all kingdoms.

William: I mentioned the practice that I do in the mirror every morning, where I go through each part of my body and I say "I love and accept this part of myself." I also ritualistically go through different parts of my body and make jokes about things that I'm insecure about.

When you're able to make yourself laugh about things that you're insecure about, you tacitly work through your problems. It also acts as an instant mood boost when you can laugh at a circumstance that is bothering you. Your laughter is a signal that you've switched your frame from a negative disposition to a positive one.

Brendon: I think that's very powerful and I think that you can see evidence for it in the fact that many comedians are people who don't quite fit in with what is classically understood in broader society as being "normal." Many stand-up comedians are people who have had personal trauma or who maybe look different or even have a physical deformity. And the reason they turn to stand-up comedy is because of the ability to make fun of themselves, make fun of their situation and reframe it in a way that gives them the feeling of control over it as well as getting the crowd's tacit acceptance and that continues their social power.

4. Pressure Flip

William: So, the last part of this section on how to take back frame is what we call a "pressure flip." Now, pressure flips are the act of flipping social pressure back on the person who put it on you. Brendon, could you actually share with us an instance that you might have had in the past?

Brendon: I just had this at work the other day because I'm in sales development, which is where business "comes from." So a lot of people in the entire organization are turning to my team to see where growth is coming from, who the new people we're doing deals with are, where is the business coming from. Recently, we've had a challenging couple of months for good reasons. One of those reasons is that we didn't have the proper product marketing tools. Many organizations in the software-as-a-service world have lots of product marketing, so they can give out flyers, videos, different things that make a case for why a prospect should meet and explore working together.

However, we didn't have any of that, so we had to generate business entirely on interpersonal interactions over email or the phone, and that's a very challenging situation to be in. The team actually succeeded because I'm a good boss and I had really good team members who worked very hard. However, I was in a meeting when the Vice President of Marketing said to me, "Hey Brendon, when are we gonna see more meetings on the board?" and I immediately pressure flipped his frame by saying "Well, when are we going to see more product marketing?" So, the frame went from "It's my responsibility to get more meetings," to "it's your responsibility to give me the tools I need to get more meetings."

William: Exactly, and this is highly effective on most people, especially when people are conflict-averse. So, if someone says "Look, I'm tired of waiting when are you going to get me your research?" And your response is "When you stop taking that tone with me." The general structure of a pressure flip is coming up with a counter frame that attacks their use of aggressive social pressure on you.

The reason why we put this tactic last is because this reframe tactics is the one that can most easily turn into a belligerent argument. When you pressure flip you must be measured.

Meaning that your tone of voice must be assertive but not aggressive. You should not label the person who is applying the pressure i.e. "You're a racist" "Misogynist" etc. and don't threaten them.

One of the things that we want to discuss is what happens when they flip the pressure back on you?

"Look, I'm tired of waiting when are you going to get me your research?"

"When you stop taking that tone with me"

"The reason I'm taking this tone is it's the only time you give me updates!"

Now, if you give in to their demands you're actually rewarding that pattern of behavior which will invite them to use it again to get what they want

So, what you say is something like "I don't like the tone of this conversation."

You want to burn that line like that into your vocabulary and practice saying it especially if people are using aggressive social pressure on you to get you to do things. What this does is it calls attention to the method they are using to extract information. It also awards you partial responsibility for the tone so that they don't lose face. It also allows you to reset the terms of engagement so that you can put yourself in a more favorable position moving forward.

If they do not accept your renewed terms, you now have a reason to implement the ignore tactic from earlier. Just think of yourself as a swordsman and you have just stated that you want to use a sword but they insist on using a machine gun. If you continue with the fight you will be putting yourself at a serious disadvantage, so rather than continue with the fight, reject the terms by refusing to engage.

Brendon: This is very important because the reframe changes the grounds under which the conversation is happening. So, Bill's example of the fighters is a good one because that's exactly what's happening; this isn't a fair fight. "Look, I'm not going to reward your behavior on interrogating me by jumping through the hoops. If you'd like to have a conversation like reasonable adults would, then you can ask me a reasonable question." That actually changes the relationship and the status between two people so that they are on even ground. If someone is displaying anger at you and demanding compliance, don't ever jump through their frame, unless they are a police officer who might shoot you, then it's probably a good idea to comply.

William: You will pick up on the fact that they are making you jump through hoops and it should ring alarm bells that this is not comfortable for you. Be careful, because this can happen very quickly. So, once again, whenever someone pressure flips you back, you can label the tone of the conversation "I don't like the tone of our conversation."

The Power Bible

Now to make it clear, the reason why you want to take partial responsibility for the tone of the conversation is because it allows them to save face. People in arguments are concerned with whether or not they are being respected, and whether or not the attribution of blame is fair.

Another tactic you can use on a re-pressure flip is ignore them and continue doing what you were doing. Know that when you do this you will inspire bad feelings from the person, so if you value the relationship, you should go back after things have cooled and talk about the subject at hand.

Brendon: The thing that you need to understand about pressure flips is that they're an attempt to inject emotion to encourage compliance in a target. The way to respond to them is by defusing the emotion and taking a higher position, which will level the two of you into a similar status.

Dismantle Their Frame

The Power Bible

F: Dismantle Their Frame

1. Logical Dismantle

William: There will be times that people will assert their worldview on you before you've had a chance to set the terms of the conversation. This is most likely to happen in an academic or workplace environment, but could also happen in a casual setting like a house party.

Now, once again, rhetoric generally beats logic in a frame battle, but being able to logically dismantle somebody's frame is the best in academic and professional environments. Generally the higher the IQ of the people you're arguing with, the more likely they are to see through an appeal to rhetoric. This is because most analysts, professionals, and professors have trained their mind to see the problems with an argument. So rhetoric is simple, but it allows for people to interpret your argument in an unfavorable light.

The first technique I learned on how to dismantle a person's frame was when I was studying for the Law School Admission Test (LSAT). What my study aid taught me was to look for the underlying assumptions in a person's argument. They did this by having you look for the assumptions in things like commercials, for example.

"If you buy 'Miracle Body Spray' girls will want to be as close to you as possible"

So right off the bat, this commercial assumes I'm heterosexual. It assumes that if I buy the body spray that I will use it. It assumes that I want girls to be close to me. It assumes that I'm single. All of these assumptions open the door for me to assert a counter argument on why not to buy the body spray.

- "I'm homosexual, I don't want women to touch me."
- "I'm in a relationship and having tons of girls around me would threaten my relationship."
- "Having girls get close to me would increase the likelihood that

I get sick."

Now, this might sound frivolous but investigating hidden assumptions in someone's pitch is a necessary part of making well informed decisions. There are times where you won't be able to do the requisite amount of research to feel comfortable before you have to make a decision. In these times, knowing what questions to ask can make all the difference. Con men and salespeople are good at representing information in such a way so that although they are not lying, they are hiding the truth. It's for this reason you have to cultivate the skill of spotting the underlying assumption in someone's answer, so that you know the next question to ask.

Another relevant instance of when knowing how to logically dismantle a person's argument is when someone in an academic or professional setting attacks you or a position that you hold. For example, if someone says "You shouldn't teach human behavior because you don't have a PhD in psychology," here is the list of assumptions in that argument and their counter argument:

- You need a PhD to teach on human behavior
  - There are many effective teachers who don't have a PhD
- You need to have studied psychology to teach on human behavior
  - Many people who understand human behavior have never   studied psychology academically.
- There are no other ways to learn about human behavior well enough to teach outside of getting a PhD
  - There are many different ways to learn enough about human behavior, such as experiences in sports, war, the workplace, etc.
- Psychology as a discipline understands social dynamics
  - There are problems with an academic approach to human   behavior

These assumptions act as a skeleton for your argument. If any of these assumptions are brought up in an argument they could deal a crippling blow to the opponent's assertion. If you can list them in rapid fire, not giving them room to respond, then you will have completely dismantled their frame logically and would leave little time for them to reassemble their frame during the course of the discussion. Caution, doing a rapid-fire dismantle will likely make that person an enemy as you have publicly made them look like a fool.

Brendon: You need to be careful because frames are emotional, frames can be backed up by facts and by logic, but frames are emotional. You do not want to fall into the trap of attempting to respond with facts or logic when the frame itself is emotional.

Let's look at global warming as an example, there are mountains of evidence to show the idea that humans have influenced the planet's atmosphere to the point that the greenhouse effect is taking place and the planet's temperature is rising due to human activity. There's a massive amount of research, something like 97 to 98 percent of any environmental scientists are in agreement that this is exactly what's taking place and temperature rise across the planet is due to human factors.

However, that isn't going to convince people who emotionally believe that it's not true. These people don't respond to facts. The people who respond to facts already have, but for those who haven't, only emotional frames will work.

William: Returning to logical dismantles, the four types of logical dismantle: 1. Use their assumptions as a place to poke holes in their argument. (mentioned above) 2. Attack the credibility of any authorities they use to uphold their argument (this can be done by looking for instances where they weren't credible, or have self-interest that makes them look unethical). Finally, 3. Utilization of Logical Fallacies

The paragon example of a person who attacks the credibility of the authorities his opponent relies on is President Trump. As we mentioned earlier, Trump labeled mainstream media as "Fake News," which allowed him to frame any information coming from them as bias and false.

The Power Bible

Although this is an extreme example the act of attacking authorities credibility is not extreme and can be done in a non-aggressive way in conversation.

The two easiest ways to attack authorities in conversation are to shine a spotlight on the incentives of the authorities, or to attack their competency. Attacking the incentives of an authority is the better strategy because it only requires you to be able to postulate what might be their incentive to hold their position, attacking their credibility for being honest.

For example, let's say someone is trying to convince me that because of global warming we are headed on a path to global omnicide, and to back up their assertion they say something like "Ninety seven percent of climatologists are in agreement that this is what is going to happen." If I respond by saying "But climatologist are the ones who have the most to *gain* by making bold predictions, as the more grim their forecast the more media attention their program will get, and the more grant money they will receive. I'm not saying they are lying, I'm just saying that they have incentive to interpret the data in a way that gets attention"

In this example, I have not called the scientists incompetent or even liars, I have just drawn attention to the fact that they have the incentive to make bold predicitions. That is more compelling than me listing statistics or attacking the competence of an entire discipline.

Attacking the competence of an authority is harder to do as it requires you to know specific instances where the authority they are relying on was wrong or incompetent, on top of the fact that if a person doesn't know about the event they can call you a liar or just say that what you mentioned was irrelevant or an outlier. Whereas, if you attack the incentives of an authority, you are having a discussion about human nature, not what happened in an isolated incident. Human nature is always relevant, difficult to argue against, and you can rely on rhetoric to make your point.

Logical Fallacies are a powerful part of a logical dismantle. They can be used as both a shield and sword, meaning they can be used to protect your argument and used as a tactic to pick apart your opponents.

An example of this is if someone attacks you or the person you are talking about without addressing your position, you can say "that's an ad hominem, you're attacking me, not my position." But let's say someone calls you out for attacking them personally and not their position, you can say "Well this is a situation where a person's character does matter, your character in this circumstance matters more than your position"

There are too many logical fallacies to go through them one by one in this book, so what we recommend is do some research and memorize them and look for them in conversation and even in advertisements.

If you use a logical fallacy and are called out, there are two general strategies for defense. The first is to say in this particular circumstance using the fallacy is justified, appealing to a moral high ground will make this strategy even more effective. The second is to call attention to the fact that the entire logical fallacy system was made up and not an official standard for discourse, and therefore irrelevant in this context.

2. Emotional Dismantle

William: A person caught up in their emotions is more likely to lose their inner frame, but it becomes more difficult for others not to comply with the external frame their enforcing.

I want you to imagine you're having an argument with somebody and they begin crying, it's difficult for you not to concede to their demands when they start crying because you feel responsible for their emotional experience.

Brendon: Not always, but in this case their crying is an attempt to reframe what you're doing to them as injury. I once dated a woman who cheated on me and when I confronted her about it, she began crying and said "why would you say these things to me?" Well, she never *denied* having done the things that I accused her of, but she was trying to reframe what I was doing to her as injury rather than confront the fact that she actually did the thing that I was accusing her of.

William: In situations like this, where you're dealing with someone crying or getting upset, if the person is angry at you or becoming violent towards you, this is a situation of duress and it's no longer about conversational frames and you should just separate yourself from the situation.

In a situation where it's not really that intense but the person you're engaging with *is* getting angry, or they are crying, you should immediately stop talking at all.

Anything that you say trying to control the situation only feeds their emotional frame of trying to get you to submit. So, if someone is getting angry at you and yelling you must not react. Maintain eye contact with a relaxed gaze. Do the same when someone begins crying. You are not responsible for anyone's emotions, but your own.

Both angry and crying people will try and provoke you if you are doing this but after a while they will run out of energy to sustain their frame. What you need to do is hold back until they have lived out the emotional cycle, the energy that it's taking to cry or be angry are difficult to sustain. Whenever the conversation restarts you will have the frame.

It's hard to do it at the moment because of the law of state transference; you feel what they feel. When you're arguing with someone who is upset, you empathize with them, and you might get angry or feel the urge to cry.

Brendon: This goes back to the definition of understanding frame control; people who react to frames are less powerful and do not control them. Instead, the frame controls *them* and not the other way around. People who do not react are the ones who control frames.

William: Their emotional outburst is one of the strongest applications of social pressure. This is a tactic to coerce you to respond and by doing nothing, the tactic doesn't work and they will be desperate for a conversational life raft.

The Power Bible

When someone comes out of an emotional state, where they completely let go and they were not validated for it, it is actually really embarrassing. That is why an angry person tries to continue to provoke you because there's nothing more embarrassing than being angry by yourself.

Brendon: And that's why they say "misery loves company."

William: Understand that a lot of the things that someone says in this state are not actually how they feel, but them using words to match their mood.

So when people are in these states they can and will say things that they know will be triggering to you. This is another reason why it's difficult to maintain frame in these situations. It is key that you understand that their emotional state is what is attacking you. That's why when you are fighting with someone they say things that can be so upsetting and hurtful and then later say "I don't know what came over me."

Knowing this will allow you not to personalize their insults. It's imperative that you do not respond to their insults because it will just give their frame energy. They are coming up with phrases to validate their emotional state, not coming up with phrases that are labelling you in a way that's accurate.

Be a person who is impossible to offend. That is how you keep frame even in the ugliest fights.

Brendon: When someone's crying at you, it doesn't necessarily mean that they're choosing, with 100 percent agency, to do this. They are trying to reframe you but many times people's emotions come from a place that they don't have control over and that could be even an evolutionary response, genetically, to input.

In the primordial past, if you, let's say, broke up with someone you were in a relationship with and told them you didn't want them in your life anymore, that could have meant life or death for them. These days, it just means you guys are going to go live separate lives surrounded by different people. However, your body doesn't know that, and that's why it responds the way that it does. That's why it's powerful for you to observe but be unresponsive to your inner feelings when things like this come up. Just allow those emotions to happen and understand that you're not attached to them, which is the same thing as being stoic.

To dismantle someone else's emotional frame. Acknowledge their emotions but do not respond to them. The goal is cooling them off, then moving toward a logical dismantle.

William: Have you ever noticed that if you ask someone "Why are you getting so mad?" even if they were not upset before they quickly become upset? That's because subconsciously they are already taking on the label you have placed on them.

This trick works in both directions. If you see someone at a party not speaking with anyone and suspect they have social anxiety then you tell them you appreciate how their calm demeanor is making you feel more calm, they will begin to act more calm. This is a dual purpose weapon as it can make your allies stronger and your enemies weaker. If you want a friend to act in a particular way just say you appreciate how they are already acting strong, calm, friendly, confident, happy, etc. If you have an enemy and want to throw them off ask them to stop being so emotional, moody, suspicious, aggressive, passive aggressive, anxious, etc. Remember that the emotion you label them with has to be within reason, or it will sound sarcastic and dishonest.

3. Group Manipulation

William: Manipulating social situations by adding more people to the group can either bring allies to your side or make you suddenly have to defend yourself against multiple attackers. It is important to know how to defend yourself against a mob, but it's also important to know how to use a mob to your advantage.

When using a group as support against someone, you should only use this on somebody that you disdain. This is not something that you want to use on even an ally or an acquaintance, but let's say your enemy is expressing a controversial opinion. Something like: "I just think we should have firmer protection on our borders."

Now, if you're within earshot of other people in the area, what you do is get their attention and say "Can you believe, he doesn't believe we should let other people immigrate into the country?!"

This creates a situation in which your opponent now must respond to a strawman argument represented to a third party who is already primed against him. This is how you create a mob against someone. This happened to me once in law school.

Brendon: When you expose it to a third party, it changes the relationship of the frame that the person has to defend. By manipulating the structure of a social situation by bringing more people into it, or cutting people out of it, it reinforces that you are the one who's in control of it and that other people are reacting to you.

William: Now, no one reading this book should actively go out and try to execute this tactic, but there are times people will do it to you, and it's best for you to know what is happening.

When this happened to me in law school, I tried to defend myself, but it wasn't working so I just stood up and walked away. I wasn't going to continue defending myself to several people because when you have several people against you, they have a collective frame which is difficult to overcome unless you have a megaphone.

What you have to do is you have to separate yourself from the situation. Now, me picking up my books and walking away probably looked weak. If I could do it again, I would have said "Hey, I don't think any of you guys are listening to what I have to say, so I'm just going to go," or "Hey, I'm not going to continue responding if you guys aren't looking to find common ground."

That would have been a more composed and dignified exit. So, if anybody ever tries to put you in a situation like this, misrepresent your political views, religious views, or something that you just said to a group that is now on you, you should say "if you actually knew my story and how I related to this, all of you would feel really bad right now," and walk away. It doesn't matter if you have a story; the fact of the matter is you make them all feel bad when you leave, that they might have actually crossed a line.

Brendon:. That tactic is reasserting "look, this is ridiculous. We're having a discussion, not a debate. If you want to have a real conversation about this, I'm happy to talk with you but otherwise, this isn't a debate on CNN."

The Power Bible

Frame Attacks

The Power Bible

How to Handle Frame Attacks

William: We've been over how to realize that you're in someone else's frame, and we've talked about how to dismantle the frames of others, and now we are going to discuss how to defend yourself when your frame gets attacked.

So, all the things tactics we discussed previously can be done back to you. As an example, let's say that Brendon is introducing his argument on why global warming is real and let's say I attack the incentives of Climatologists.

How you should deal with a logical attack is actually with rhetoric. If you keep trying to use logic, it will be the person with the most facts that takes the frame. That's how people like Ben Shapiro win debates so easily, because he has researched his positions far more deeply than the people he's arguing against. Instead you want to shift away and move toward a different rhetorical field

So, if I say to Brendon "well, how do you know that climatologists aren't exaggerating to get more money for their research?" Brendon could say "look, academia and the scientific method lifted us out of the dark ages. I have no trouble putting my trust in that community."

Here's an easy rhetorical tool. If someone logically attacks your frame, if you zoom out, you're looking at the big picture; if you zoom in, you're focusing on a technicality that they're not addressing. Those are the two ways you can shield yourself from a logical attack. When you zoom in, to a technical difference you have to connect that technicality to a principle that's easy for people to jump on board with, like "Justice" or "Equality."

When you zoom out, you make things about the larger picture, it can be something aspirational or something we want to avoid. Watch political debates and panel discussions, these methods are the go-to in avoiding addressing the actual problem. If someone tries to zoom out on you, say something like

"Let's not get lost in the bigger picture, the details matter," and if they try and zoom in on you say "You're getting lost in the details; you're missing the forest for the trees."

Brendon: If someone is attacking your frame, and you find yourself actually getting emotional, the best move is to just check out.

You should take a second, close your eyes, take a deep breath, remind yourself that this is just a conversation, feel your feet on the ground, count to 10 and then you'll calm down enough to think logically and rationally. If you have to, walk away. You can just say "you know what, I've gotta leave this conversation, I'm too attached right now, I don't want to say anything I don't mean." These are all good ways to have excuses to back up and give yourself some space.

William: Notice that Brendon didn't say "I'm angry," he said, "I'm attached." He didn't say "I'm sad," he said that "I'm attached" to the outcome. Saying that you're just too attached to the argument or "I get too passionate about this topic." If you're the first to label your emotion, you are more in control of the subsequent narrative. So rather than being characterized as belligerent, you're passionate about this particular issue. One is a virtue while the other is a vice.

Brendon: You can say, "this topic is really important to me, so I get pretty worked up about it and I don't want to say anything I don't mean, so I think I'm just going to take a second to calm down a little bit."

William: This book is about how to win the conversations that matter. So, if you're in a situation that matters and you find yourself upset, even if it's in a negotiation, take time to walk out before you have terms that aren't favourable to you placed on you because you are in that emotional state.

Status Attack

William: Status attacks are when someone attempts to diminish your credibility by calling attention to an indicator of status that you lack.

The Power Bible

So if you're asserting an argument and someone says, "Wait, where did you go to school?" You should respond by saying some form of "Is that relevant?"

Brendon: Many people fall into the trap of thinking that symbols of authority or credibility trump the point of the argument.

William: People feel urged sometimes to justify themselves when this happens. For example, I could say "I have a Juris Doctorate," or "Brendon graduated college with honors in philosophy," but the second you try to justify yourself to them you're already feeding into their frame. Justifying yourself and attempting to name your bona fides is a mistake because they're attempting to frame *themselves* as the authority of what is credible and what isn't. You're never going to come up as enough by their valuation no matter what you say. There is no weaker frame than the frame of trying to convince someone because it leaves the power in *their* hands to validate your frame.

Brendon: You should never try to "convince" anyone of anything. It only serves to reinforce that you don't have status in comparison to them. People in positions of authority tend *not* to explain themselves to others. This doesn't mean you should *never* explain yourself, but you should exercise discretion as to when and how you choose to do this.

William: Another type of status attack is where someone attacks a feature about you implying that it's low status. This could be something as simple as talking about how you're dressed, or it could be something as aggressive as saying something racist or classist.

In these instances, you have to remember our statement about having the inner frame of someone who is impossible to offend. So even if they say something offensive, do not allow it to shake you. Remember that the easier you are to offend the less confident you are, therefore the weaker frame you have. If the slight was made as a joke, then laugh it off and bolster yourself.

Frame Addiction

The Power Bible

Frame Addiction

William: Frame addiction is when someone feels the need to control the conversation, in every conversation, even in instances where they do not have authority. Their pursuit of conversational control can come at a great cost as they will alienate the people around them in order to get and sustain control.

People who are most likely to suffer from frame addiction are people who must negotiate for a living (salespeople, trial attorneys, etc.), people whose job requires them to be in a position of authority (Police officers, managers, etc.), and people who are often amongst the most important people in the room (CEO, celebrities, etc.).

Trial attorneys and salespeople can be affected by this because to be good at their job they must be good at asserting their frame on people. There are consequences for them losing frame such as not winning the case or losing the sale.

But there are circumstances outside of the courtroom: dealing with colleagues, dealing with their spouses, dealing with kids, social gatherings like book clubs where someone doesn't need to be in control. Yet, frame addicts find themselves attempting to take control of every situation and try to make others submit to their frame.

This is exhausting because most people don't like being around people who need to dominate the conversation. If you're a frame addict, you'll end up with others not wanting to be around you, or resisting your frame whenever you do have a good idea. Basically, you'll lose friends and make enemies.

One of the easiest ways to see if someone is a frame addict is to watch how they react when they do not have the frame. Do they get upset. Feign aloofness. Raise their voice. Walk out of the room. Sulk. These are all ways that a frame addict reacts when they are not at the center of attention or they have anyone stand up against them.

Brendon: Frame addiction can result in you misperceiving social situations as always having a winner and loser. Normally, interactions do not have any sum; they're just an open-ended infinite game. Most people don't appreciate being around others who suddenly start treating normal conversation as a contest.

This is a huge problem that people who first learn about frames can tend to develop. I know that when I first learned about frames, I walked around deconstructing anything anybody said to me as a frame battle and how they were pursue out-framing me. It's not a good way to live your life. It's not productive, and it can lead to conversations that are uncomfortable for yourself and for others. Doing this can actually cause you to ruin social relationships you have had for a long time.

William: Being hyper-aware of who has frame all the time can actually make *you* lose frame. It makes you cultivate a sensitivity that creates insecurity. The amount of information you're taking in will make you feel more anxious because you're trying to interpret too much information at once.

This is why it's important to have a strong inner frame. The stronger your inner frame the more effortless it will be for you to have frame. That way you can stay focused on relevant information and also be able to properly police yourself, allowing others to have their moment.

Validating The Frames of Others

William: People like when you validate their frame, it feels very good to have somebody agree with you. That's why people tend to do it, because it helps to win friends and influence people, but there is a problem with being too agreeable.

The more that you validate somebody's frame the less authority they're going to give you over them. I want you to imagine somebody you meet at a party. At the beginning of the conversation they compliment you once or twice, but then as the night goes on, they're complimenting you on everything. Then this person tries to convince you of something, doesn't matter what it is, but they ask for your compliance. Suddenly, you feel a wall inside you go up.

This happens because you don't feel, deep down, that you've *earned* any of these compliments. So when they ask for a small amount of compliance your defense mechanisms go up. They've given you a lot of validation that you haven't earned, you feel the deficit.

We don't recommend you do this to others, instead what we would recommend doing is making people earn your approval but then validate them wholeheartedly after they put in the work.

So, if you're in a discussion with someone and you have opposing viewpoints, even if you see what somebody's saying, have them explain more of their point and then say "You know what? After thinking about it, I actually really do agree with you." Even if you wanted to agree with them from the beginning, make them wait for your validation by taking the time to look reflective.

By suspending your agreement, you can actually build more peer authority with a person by making them prove their point; they will implicitly respect you and also enjoy having you around because you're still validating their frame.

Brendon: What other things would you say are dangers of frame addiction?

William: Applying the wrong game in the wrong circumstances is a big danger. Your arguments in your private life aren't about winning or losing, they're about solving problems, but whenever you take the orientation of "I am going to win!" in a situation where the goal isn't to win, you end up getting the results that you don't want.

I had one professor at my law school – who was an accomplished DA, and he ended up telling me in one of our close conversations that the skills that he cultivated as a DA were what destroyed his marriage.

He could not turn off the need to win every conversation. There's an Alain De Botton quote, "If you win every argument with your spouse, you won't be married and they won't be your spouse in three years."

Brendon: Once again, the ultimate frame is the fun frame and it shows that you're high status and that you're enjoying yourself. No one can resist it. It's the ultimate skeleton key to social situations. If you're constantly analyzing frames, seeing who's winning or losing, you're not going to be fun, you're not going to be in the moment, and you're going to be trying to win.

William: If you're often in a position of authority and you find yourself in a position where you don't have authority, sometimes your brain doesn't account for the difference. You can perceive someone's aloofness as a direct attack; them standing up for themselves as undermining you.

Brendon: Another side effect of this that we know from experience is when your frame is refused, or when it's broken, or when there's another frame that outframes yours, you can experience negative feelings. If you're constantly focused on only winning frame battles or outframing everyone else because you're addicted to frames, then you're going to be feeling negative emotions often because people can casually disregard your frames in normal conversation because the stakes are very low. As a result you can feel negative and blow yourself out of social situations. Bill and I were at an exclusive party in the south of France—not bragging, that was just true.

William: Ha, ha, it's not bragging, they're just facts.

Brendon: We were at a party in the south of France and a semi-famous actor was trying to talk with some girls that Bill and I were chatting with. Bill had such a strong, fun frame that when this famous actor came up and tried to talk to them, they didn't even acknowledge him.

The girls talking with Bill just ignored this actor; they ignored his implicit authority and status because the *actual* fun Bill was generating was greater than the *potential* fun that this *not* fun actor was trying to generate with them.

The actor actually got very frustrated and left. That's frame addiction.

What could have happened very easily is that the actor could have just vibed with Bill, made friends with us, and then joined the group and *then* could have led the fun.

William: He wasn't the center of attention in this circumstance, which bothered him. What bothered him even more was that the girls already knew that he was famous! This guy, for all intents of purposes, was taller, better looking and more accomplished than me. He actually beat me in every way we discussed to have implicit authority in a situation.

Brendon: True, but he wasn't generating as much fun, and because he was addicted to having the authority frame he didn't have anything else to do, so he left.

William: The last thing to talk about regarding frame addiction is frame imbalanced relationships. There are certain relationships where we're pliant individuals, but there are other relationships we have in life where we're used to holding the frame.

This could be in a master-mentor relationship, father & son, older sister & younger sister, etc, it could even be a romantic relationship or just a friendship where you are the more dominant one.

You can have frame addiction in a relationship to a point where if a person breaks rapport with you just by expressing themselves, you perceive this as disrespect. This happens a lot in sibling rivalries. It can happen when a younger sibling comes into their own and it causes discord within the family.

You want to be aware of relationship in which you are the leader. How do you deal with someone disagreeing with you? Are you the first one to raise your voice in the fight? Is it easy for them to provoke you into displays of anger?

Brendon: Especially, you'll notice this reaction when you're in a situation in which you know that you're *supposed* to be having fun but you're not having it. If you can identify places in your life where you know that you are *supposed* to be having fun—to be clear, not "I'm in Las Vegas and I'm not having fun," but "I'm with my wife and I'm not having fun. I'm not enjoying it" or "I'm with my friends and I'm not enjoying it"—the first thing you should do is look at yourself in those situations and ask "What are the things I'm bringing to the table that are impairing me or others from having a good time right now?" If you're feeling you need to be the center of attention, or you need to be in control, that indicates frame addiction.

William: Exactly. Look for places where you're reluctant to express why you're upset or thinking phrases like "They disrespected me' in your mind. This is often evidence that you are uncomfortable with them voicing their opinion because you are addicted to the frame in that particular relationship.

Solutions to Frame Addiction

William: Frame addicts take themselves seriously. Many times they have a hard time being teased. This is because many frame addicts don't have a dynamic frame. Rather, they have a rigid frame. As we mentioned earlier in the book, it's easier to have a strong frame when it's rigid but it leads to bad results down the line.

So part of the solution for being a frame addict is to notice when you're being domineering and take a moment to laugh at yourself. If you were being disagreeable don't be afraid of apologizing.

Hey, you know, I kinda overdid that you know, my bad." Or "Guys, I've been monopolizing the conversation. I am so sorry, you were saying?

People will give you leeway when you have self-awareness. Look for cues that you're being domineering. Are you interrupting people a lot? Are you talking loud? Are you talking loudly to make other people be quiet? Are you putting your hands all over somebody whenever they're trying to express their point?

These are all ways that you can see that you're trying to assert your frame on somebody, but if it's in a situation where you don't have to assert your frame, then you are wasting social capital on winning conversations that don't matter.

Brendon: Bill's right. Just apologize briefly and say, "I'm sorry, I'm in work mode. I apologize. Let me just kind of come down from that."That's you might need to do to win people back over.

William: We also want you to inspect your past. Were there people you use to be close with but you started getting angry with them for merely stating their opinions and now you guys aren't close? Ask yourself "Was I addicted to having the frame in this relationship?" If that was the case, maybe give them a call.

"Hey, you know I got mad at you and said you were disrespecting me as the reason but looking back I wasn't letting you grow into your own person. I got used to being the person in control and you growing scared me. I apologize for any friction that might've caused our relationship"

Breaking Rules

Brendon: Let's talk about the second danger of frame control, which is breaking rules. This comes second to frame addiction even though it is actually the more immediate danger to you in your life. One of the things that we've mentioned throughout this book is that when you know that controlling frame can allow you to bend or even break some rules, some people are apt to toss the entire rule book out the window and just move ahead with the idea that they can do whatever they want in their life. This is very dangerous for obvious reasons. One of the last things you can try to do is break the rules with the police, is how you end up shot. I'm only laughing because that's just true.

William: This book is meant to teach you the art of bending, not breaking rules. Even though all rules are made up, breaking certain rules can have severe consequences. So you have to operate with restraint. If there is a rule or law that is a barrier between you and what you want, look for a way to finesse the rule rather than break it.

The Power Bible

You can't just cut the line in front of a club, you have to have a purpose. That purpose could be paying the bouncer, talking to the bouncer about how long the wait is, asking what their dress code rules are, etc. Get good at investigating the consequences of certain actions. Try testing the limits of what we call "soft rules" which are rules with no clear consequence or where the consequence is just a verbal warning like, "Don't do that."

That being said, walking into Barnes and Noble, taking a book and walking out of the store is just straight-up stealing, and can lead to you being detained or going to jail. Your defense can't be "Well the price is arbitrarily determined, money isn't real, and we're all part of an imaginary game," that defense will not work. Once again, although the game is made up, it has real consequences.

Brendon: The way you bend the rules is by operating within the rules to start, and then getting the implicit buy-in from people who are meant to enforce the rules. That way, it's okay for you to be outside the boundaries of the rules.

A good example of this comes from when I was working with a dating coach, one of the best in the world, he challenged me one day to go into a candy store and walk out with free samples. There was no free sample sign. There was no offer of free samples. He just said, "Just go in and get as many free samples as you can get."

That's the kind of way that you need to think about bending rules. I didn't just walk in and grab a candy and leave. I walked in and convinced people who had implicit authority to give me something for free.

You're not breaking the rules. You're bending the rules because the people who have the power to influence or assert the rules are giving you room to go outside the bounds of the rules.

William: The first time James Altucher and I hung out he told me if I go to the store and buy something, I should ask if I can get that item for cheaper. I tried it at a pharmacy and they actually gave a coupon discount on some of the items I was purchasing just because I asked.

Brendon: That's 100% true. So one of the biggest dangers to this is just a straight out breaking the rules and going over lines that really shouldn't be crossed. As you know from this book, frame control operates in spaces in which value is ambiguous. At a store, we're not really sure exactly who has the authority.

If you've worked in a store you've heard the adage, "The customer is always right." So who has the authority at the cash register? Is it the manager or is it the customer? Because if the customer has some authority, they can use that authority to enforce a frame on the situation that is to their benefit.

The people who run the store want to make a sale as much as the customer wants to purchase something. So situations like that are malleable enough that someone who has a very strong frame can enforce it.

Perception, Sociopathy, and Machiavellianism.

William: What we have taught you are the rules of the game. After reading this book you will notice things about others. You will stand up for yourself in ways most people don't. Most of all, you will understand why things are the way they are and that makes people suspicious.

Talking about the lessons from this book in casual conversations could earn you the label of sociopath or a machiavellian deceiver. I say this because people say this about me. I recently put up a poll on my Instagram asking my followers who believe I'm a sociopath, and an overwhelming majority hit "Yes."

There is an inherent distrust of people who understand how to manipulate the emotions of others to get what they want. That's why we recommend not bringing up what we have taught you with acquaintances. They will not be impressed, they will be suspicious.

Questions like "Are we having a real discussion right now? Are you implementing one of your frame control tactics?" will come up, people will be more on-guard. The tactics we've taught you will have less of an effect. You will be watched like an audience watching a magician, looking for the trick.

So we implore you to be restricted with who you share what you've learned with. Recommend the book, but don't be the one who's giving the lessons.

Brendon: This was a mistake that I made when I first started learning about frame control. I thought that I could claim some social value by looking intelligent, by explaining to everyone the situation that they were in and what they were doing. Unfortunately it didn't work, it just sounded strange and weird. You don't want to make that mistake.

The truth is also that you shouldn't be walking around thinking this way all the time. It's the same thing as frame addiction.

Part of what is joyful in life is having people who you meet like you authentically. If you're constantly thinking about frames and attempting to win and outmaneuver everyone in a conversation, you're never going to trust someone's actual feelings for you.

William: There is a reversal of this as well. If you regularly have had people take advantage of you, then flaunt your knowledge. People will be less likely to fuck with you if they think you have the capacity to be evil. It's not what you do, it's what people think you might do that gives you power.

Brendon: In other words, don't fly your colors immediately.

William: Be aware when you're amongst other Machiavellian types. When amongst sharks, don't be afraid to signal that you are one too.

Brendon: I think an explanation might be useful for someone reading this.

William: For example, let's say that you are in the middle of negotiations and they want to have several of their people on the call. Don't be afraid to signal that you know having that many people on a call is a tactic the other side is playing.

"Why do you need this many people on the call?"

"Looking at the list of people on this call, I'm going to feel more comfortable if we have a couple members from my team on this call as well; add Brendon to the call"

By signaling that you know that their behavior is a tactic, they will be less likely to take you seriously. In the example above, the more people on a call that are on the opposing team, the more easily they can outframe you, as they will just appeal to the other people in the call to validate their frame. Because you have less support on the call, you will be more likely to take less than you deserve. Many negotiators understand this intuitively and will stack the call with unnecessary people to create an echo chamber during the negotiation.

In circumstances like these, don't be afraid to utilize validation vacuums or imply that you are suspicious of certain behaviors. Subtly calling awareness to behavior that you find suspicious early on will make them less likely to try something duplicitous later on, as you have signaled to them that you are vigilant and comfortable addressing incongruencies.

Remember that tension is a natural part of negotiation as well, and being averse to creating any will result in you having a difficult time getting the outcome you want. So don't worry about making things awkward or tense during these moments as most people who are regularly involved in negotiations have a high capacity to deal with the feelings of tension and rarely hold grudges after an agreement has been reached.

When signaling, context and depth are two important things to think about. For example, let's imagine that Brendon and I have been traveling all day and he hasn't eaten in 10 hours. If while we are arguing and I explain to Brendon the reason why he's upset is actually because he hasn't eaten in 10 hours, has felt out of control because we've spent the entire day traveling, and he's predisposed to getting upset in these circumstances because it makes him feel like a child, then, frustrated with these feelings, he is lashing out on me because I'm the only person around and he knows he can repair the damage done later because we're close friends, he's going to feel creeped out.

Brendon: You should remember the human fallibility principle. Just because you get the feeling that somebody might be doing something for such-and-such a reason, it doesn't mean that that's true. It could be, but you could be wrong. So operate under the idea that at any moment you could get some disconfirming information and should let go of your previous belief.

William: People want to control other people's actions and that is impossible. What we are teaching is to control emotions. Our emotions control our actions. So if you make someone feel an emotion that matches the action you want them to carry out, you increase the likelihood of them carrying out that action.

Brendon: I think that's really well said.

Coercion

Brendon: Coercion is defined as "The practice of persuading someone to do something by using force or threats."

William: Coercion builds resentment. The definition mentions force and threat. Threatening people is an extreme form of coercion but it's not the way it manifests. The more common form of coercion is the application of social force with a combative tone, aggressive stance, and being hyper persistent after a person has already stated that they do not want to do what you are trying to force them to do. This type of behavior erodes the relationship.

Brendon: This is true is because of cognitive dissonance in the brain.

If someone can assign a reason for why they did a behavior, they're going to assign it to whatever's most immediately and easily available. So if someone acts only because they feel coerced to do so, they are accepting your frame, they are responding to a threat.

The Power Bible

William: A true master of frame control makes people believe that what they are doing is for their own best interest. Remember that coercion doesn't always look insidious and aggressive. Sometimes coercion happens when you're the center of attention and everyone is laughing and having a good time. Sometimes people have had a wonderful time being your frame the whole night, doing what you say, but eventually, that can build resentment because at times everyone wants to be a star.

Brendon: This happened to me when I was dating a woman who saw that I used to get a lot of phone calls from a female friend of mine. I've been friends with this woman for years. The woman who I was dating recognized how close my friend and I were and she got threatened.

So my girlfriend put a lot of pressure on me to delete my friend's phone number and not speak with her. After a while under this pressure, I finally relented to it. However, it ended up backfiring because I was more frustrated at my girlfriend and she was more frustrated at me because she had to coerce me in order to get me to do something rather than me doing it on my own volition.

William: Exactly. It's kind of like putting a gun to somebody's head and asking them if they love you.

Brendon: That's the most extreme example, but it is still a good example.

William: They would have loved you in other circumstances, but they felt forced into it.

Brendon: And either way you've ruined the relationship.

Dangers of Frame

Brendon: One of the things that you should be aware of when you begin using frame control and get decent at it, is that your status is going to grow and as your status grows, you're going to be presented with new and more uniquely challenging situations. That's just the way that it's going to be.

People who used to be allies of yours are now going to be competitors and enemies, and people who were enemies of yours previously are now going to be supplicants. Former enemies of yours might end up trying to be friends only to undermine you. The world around you is going to change its relationship to you because you've changed your relationship to yourself, and because you change your relationship to it.

Something that you very seriously need to be aware of is the fact that tactics that worked previously will no longer work moving forward. People who you used to apologize to previously and everything was fine, now will no longer accept your apology.

This is a danger of frame control; through the ability to control frames at your office, you could earn a promotion that could put you in a bad situation, and then you could be fired. You could be let go because you failed to respect the fact that you've gained new enemies who wanted you off the chessboard.

So as you ascend and use more frame control, exercise more frame control and get better at actually improving your life, you need to recognize that new and different challenges will present themselves to you. The only way for you to have confidence to face them is have faith in yourself and accept that you may fail, but you will continue to fight and exercise your best ability to influence frames around you and improve your life.

William: I love this. I would just add this, the faster you ascend, the more people will declare you as enemies.

Brendon: Yes. A classic phrase is "game recognizes game."

William: As your status rises from employing the techniques mentioned in this book you will notice that you will start to treat people differently. There will be places where this change in behavior is appropriate, like treating people who use to be co-workers like employees after a promotion.

The Power Bible

That being said, your promotion at work should not change how you treat your friends *outside* of work. Yet, this can happen because we get used to the increase in status in one area and think that the privilege of authoritative behavior extends outside of that particular place.

Having a strong inner frame is to be confident and self-aware at the same time. Be wary of yourself when bathing in the validation of others. Those who allow themselves to get drunk on the praise from a victory are more likely to stumble into failure.

Robert Greene says, "Stop after you've achieved victory." After you've already gotten what you want, do not go farther just for the sake of going farther without having a plan. Because remember, once again, we can't say this enough, the faster you ascend, the more enemies you cultivate.

So enjoy victories, but remain vigilant, of yourself, and those close to you. Remember that Caesar's ascent was what turned his best friend into his assassin.

Brendon: When a Roman general achieved a great victory, he would be granted a great parade known as a triumph. At the culmination of his triumph a laurel crown would be placed on the general's head. At that moment a slave would whisper in his ear "sic transit gloria." In English, "glory fades."

The danger is hubris. The classic sense of hubris is pride in the face of the gods. To you, this means that you believe that you're above consequences; that because of how much you believe in yourself, nothing bad will ever happen to you.

It's important to understand that hubris is a kind of overwhelming self-belief that occurs outside of one's competence or ability to exercise proper judgment. People who have an enormous amount of confidence, but no skill to back it up are headed for disaster every time.

William: A problem people have when they achieve success is to over attribute their success to themselves. The reason why you should not praise yourself after victory isn't because it's off putting but because it obscures your ability to see what actually made you successful. Always survey the context around your success for the truth.

The Power Bible

The Power Link

Conclusion

The Power Bible

In his short masterwork Managing Oneself, Peter Drucker says that one must begin with the question "What do I want my contribution to be?" It's true, one must begin there, but to truly answer that, one must also see what's possible. Only after one *believes* that they have the power to make a contribution, can the vision of a contribution be seen.

The investigation of power seeks to answer the question "What can I do?" As every human has the ability to choose good or evil things, we ask you to answer the question with good choices.

The world is indifferent, apathetic, unkind and often unforgiving. Having power means the ability to affect meaningful change in the world. Power allows you to create space for yourself, and for others, and within that space to influence the values and quality of life for all those people.

You have the power to improve the well being of yourself and of those around you.

Along the path, pursuing the contribution you want to make, you'll encounter pitfalls, challenges, and trials. You'll find yourself in new situations that you haven't been prepared for. You'll feel fear, exhilaration, even excitement. As you try new things, have new experiences and end up in situations you've never been in before keep one thing in mind: Trust yourself.

The process of self discovery, the pathway to power, is a journey of self discovery, and the journey of self discovery is a journey of self trust. Using this book as a guide, you'll start where the words end, learning how you operate with others, what works for you, what works on you. This book could never be so complete as to know what *your* pathway to power is, so you must complete it.

Every day, wake up and greet the unknown with a promise that you'll find the pathway, or you'll make one. Power lies in the *actions* you take after *deciding* to take them. Do this, every day, and you'll take your place in the halls of history among the greatest who have ever been. As insurmountable as achieving your goals can sometimes feel, as hopeless as life can sometimes seem, grasping real power comes from continuing the commitment to action even in these moments. When it looks like nothing will work out, and nothing is certain, this is the time to trust in yourself.

Trust in yourself, trust in your actions, trust in your commitment to gain power and you will. Life is built from stumbles and picking yourself back up. Continue, and grasp the power you want to change your life.

"To those human beings who are of any concern to me I wish suffering, desolation, sickness, ill-treatment, indignities—I wish that they should not remain unfamiliar with profound self-contempt, the torture of self-mistrust, the wretchedness of the vanquished: I have no pity for them, because I wish them the only thing that can prove today whether one is worth anything or not—that one endures."
- Friedrich Nietzsche

Postscript

Postscript

The gardener grows with his garden. This author grew with his book. A year ago I started writing this book. Heartbroken and shattered. Putting pen to page forced me to learn lessons I had once known but had forgotten.

There will be parts of this book that you will hope to remember but forget.
There will be parts of the book you will practice, experience results, then quit.
There will be insecurities that you will believe you have conquered, that will return on a different day.

In dark times,

Let this book be your guide.
When sadness accompanies every sunrise.
When you have convinced yourself that you do not know the way.
Let this book remind you who you once were,

And more importantly,

Who that person believed you could be.

Like writing The Power Bible has done for me.

-Will

Printed in Great Britain
by Amazon